John G. Walla

History in the Hills
Walks in the Corbetts and Donalds

'History in the Hills – Walks in the Corbetts and Donalds'
Copyright © John G. Wallace, Edinburgh 2000

First published in Great Britain in 2000 by
        Shona Low
        Thornfield
        Erskine Loan
        Gullane. EH31 2EH

ISBN: 0-9539268-0-X

Front Cover: William Wallace at Bemersyde

Title page: The Cobbler from Arrochar
        Photo: Alistair Low

Photos and maps: John Wallace
Book design and production: Shona Low
Printed by David MacDonald Ltd, 25 Rodney Street, Edinburgh, EH7 4EL

This book is dedicated to my many walking companions over the years. I have greatly valued their friendship and hope that they will enjoy the historical associations I have attached to the walks.

This book would not have been printed without the help of my daughter, Shona, and to her I am especially grateful.

Contents

Foreword

      It was with some personal astonishment that I completed the ascent of the Munros after I retired, as I had for many years given up hope of ever succeeding. I started by climbing Lochnagar with my Father in 1931 and finished with Carn Liath in 1983 accompanied by 3 of my children and their spouses and 8 of my grandchildren.

      In the distant pre-war years I enjoyed hill walking and was beginning to enjoy rock climbing but I returned from the war to civil life with a spinal disability. Although I managed the occasional ascent of a Munro I had not seriously contemplated finishing the list as I felt that my unpredictable cramp would preclude me from climbing the Skye Munros. However, following the death of my wife a few years after I retired, I felt the need of a definite objective and for this, a list of mountains to climb was ideal. I am not a great believer in lists of hills to be climbed as there are some superb hills which are not included in any of the lists- but for some purposes the existence of a list is suitable.

1

Foreword

_____

I undertook a period of training to see if I could stand up to a few years of serious hill walking. I was gratified to find that after a few weeks I had little trouble with my spinal difficulty and was able to satisfy myself as to a reasonable degree of fitness.

I decided to try to complete the list of Munros of which I had climbed over 100 in pre-war days. On completion of the Munros I was in my seventieth year but felt that I was still fit enough for a few more years active hill- walking. I elected to try to complete the list of Corbetts and Donalds as in the Scottish Mountaineering Guide Book. I was fortunate, I may say, as after completion of the Scottish lists I was still able to enjoy the McGillicuddy Reeks and other 3000 foot mountains in Ireland and, much to my delight, the splendid Welsh 3000 foot mountains with their magnificent ridge walks.

Corbetts and the Donalds

To an increasingly large number of people the Munros are well known. They are the hills included in the 'List of Heights over 3000 feet' compiled by Sir Hugh Munro in 1891, and since then adjusted in the light of more up-to-date surveying and further exploration.

Corbett's Tables and, even more so, Donald's Tables have not yet attained the same familiarity as have the Munros and I therefore give a short description of their coverage.

The fourth man to climb all the Munros in Sir Hugh's original list was J.Rooke Corbett who completed them in 1930. In addition to climbing all the Tops over 3000 feet he had ascended all the 2500 foot mountains but he did not publish his list of these 2500 feet hills himself. The list was eventually passed on to the Scottish Mountaineering Club by his sister after his death. There was no indication in the papers passed over as to how he had selected the mountains but examination of the list made it clear that his criterion was that there should be an ascent of at least 500 feet to the summit in every direction. He did not take into account any question of difficulty or of accessibility. The list of Corbetts, as the mountains have come to be known, has been reassessed in the light of up-to-date surveys and other considerations, as have the Munros, and, as a result, the number of Corbetts stands at 224.

Donald's Tables were produced by Percy Donald and are based on somewhat different criteria from those used by Corbett. His list includes all hills in the Scottish Lowlands over 2000 feet in height. Donald visited every hill himself at least once before he included it in his list.

The list is divided into three classes. 'Tops' are summits with an ascent of at least 100 feet in any direction although Donald included a number of summits of topographical merit where he reduced the 100 feet to

50 feet. Having specified the 'Tops' he then grouped them into 'Hills', his primary classification, with their associated 'Tops', adopting the criterion that a 'Top' had to be within about one and a half miles of the main summit of the group and have an ascent of at least 50 feet from its connecting col. He had a final subsidiary group, 'Points', in which he included all summits where a height of 2000 feet was exceeded but which could not rank as either a 'Hill' or a 'Top'. The Scottish Lowlands extend from the Cheviots to the Ochils, but for completeness the ranking hills of the Cheviots which are in England have been enumerated. As with the other lists, up-to-date survey and closer examination have resulted in some change from Donald's original list. There are now, in Scotland, 88 'Hills', 139 'Tops' and 28 'Points'. As already mentioned, the list also specifies the 5 Cheviot hills which are in England which if included would raise the number of 'Hills' and 'Tops' each by 5.

Scottish History

I have always been interested in the history of Scotland particularly after the abandonment of the Antonine Wall by the Romans at the beginning of the third century. It was at this time that the unification of the country into the Scotland we now know effectively began.

The country was then occupied by five different peoples. The Picts occupied the area of Scotland stretching from the Forth to the Moray Firth. The Scots, who emigrated from Ireland, occupied what is approximately the county of Argyll. In the west, the Britons occupied the area south of the Antonine Wall to the line of Hadrian's Wall which was the Roman boundary at the time. The Angles occupied the territory of what is now Northumberland up to the Forth estuary. Lastly the Norsemen controlled the Hebrides and the major part of North Scotland including the Orkneys and Shetlands. The main stages of the unification took several centuries to complete.

Scope of this book

In the course of my walks among the Corbetts and the Donalds I covered country associated with many of the great historical events of the nation. I found it fascinating, wherever possible, to link my walks with historical events which took place in their neighbourhood. Some of these historical events may not be supported by firm facts but there is usually some suggestive evidence to support what looks like, in any event, a probable occurrence.

In the book, I have selected a group of important Scottish historical events and have briefly put each one in its context in the history of the nation. I have then associated with each one the Donalds and Corbetts in the geographical locations concerned and have described the actual walks.

The historical events selected and the hills I have associated with each of the events are shown in the Chronological Summary.

Planning the walks

Being over 70, the project of climbing about 200 hills of different degrees of accessibility and difficulty over a limited period of years - amid my other activities - required reconsideration of my physical condition which had been quite adequate for the Munros. I had myself medically re-examined and was assured of my fitness to undertake the physical effort.

As I would likely be walking on my own on numerous occasions and as I was concerned that I should not cause unnecessary problems to other people by getting into difficulty which could have been avoided, I felt that I should make some personal rules particularly for these occasions.

The only weather conditions which would require special care were snow and ice as I am not experienced in the use of crampons and ice axe. I also find that I now become excessively cold very quickly. Therefore, if I was unaccompanied, my snow walks would have to be undertaken in fine conditions only. Severe rain or mist would not in themselves keep me from the objective but as my dog was still young, I would have to plan carefully for any likely difficult stream crossings in spate. In practice this problem only troubled me once where although I crossed a rapidly flowing stream well over knee depth I could not get my dog to follow me. This problem did not last long as he very quickly learned to like the water and became an excellent swimmer.

It is sensible for all parties to leave a note as to the proposed route in the hills and the expected time of return but it is particularly important to do this at older ages if one is walking alone. I therefore made it a rule when on my own, to leave a note in my car, tent or bothy, of my expected route and timings and also of any 'escape' route I might decide to follow in the event of difficulty.

Problems of access

In planning my walks, I benefited by reading descriptions of the routes adopted by leading mountaineering writers such as Tom Weir, Hamish Brown (whose excellent book on the Corbetts was not available at the time), Rennie MacOwan, and others and this was not only interesting but helpful. Nevertheless I went my own way - by no means guaranteed to be the most desirable or the most interesting. It was usually selected because it was the route starting as near to the mountain base as possible. Sometimes however it was not possible to get anywhere near the start of the climbing and I then tried to find a route where I could make use of my folding cycle

Foreword

which I carried in the boot of my car.

After planning a route, I tried where practicable to speak to the keeper or farmer over whose country I would be walking. When I managed to do this, I found it most useful as, not only did I ensure that I was not interfering with estate activities or other sporting events such as stalking or shooting, but I invariably obtained valuable information about the ground I proposed to cover. There were only rare occasions when the keeper told me that, according to the owners instructions, there was no access permitted. Usually however access from another direction could be found enabling me, I must confess, to enjoy the satisfaction of circumventing the really quite unnecessary veto.

It is surprising how often I had difficulty in finding out who was the person who was responsible for the ground I was going to cross. At that time there was a file available giving the names and addresses of landowners and their local representatives. Although I found this helpful there were numerous areas where it was not easy to find the local contact. I feel that if a more comprehensive record could be prepared and made available for consultation at the local post office or police station, many of the problems would be overcome particularly with respect and understanding from both occupiers of the ground and their representatives and from those desiring access. I am not a supporter of unqualified rights of access nor of confrontational methods associated with attempts to obtain access. Nevertheless I am a practiser of responsible freedom of access. I am also a strong supporter of the Scottish Rights of Way Society and I would be very much in favour of a broadening of some of their activities, if this could be made legally and financially possible, to include general problems of freedom of access.

Chronological Summary

Date	Historical episode	Monarch	Hills
	Spread of Christianity		
	St Ninian		Fleet Hills
	St Donnan		Sail Mhor
	St Maelrubha		Applecross, Loch Clair Great Wilderness, Loch Vaich
	Unification of Scotland		
685	Nechtansmere		Mount Battock
1018	Carham	Malcolm II	Cheviots
1034	Strathclyde	Duncan I	Rhinns of Kell
1040	Galloway	Macbeth	Dungeon Hills
	Somerled and the Norsemen		
1120		Alexander I	Hills of Morvern
1153		David I	Ardgour
1263	**Haakon and the Battle of Largs**		
		Alexander III	Northern Hills, Knoydart
	Wars of Independence		
1291	Wallace	John Balliol	Ettrick Hills, Pass of Brander
1314	Bruce	Robert I	Glen Trool & Minigaff Hills
1332	Edward Balliol	David II	Morven (Culblean Hill)
1500	**Foot Pilgrimage of James IV**		
		James IV	Tinto, Culter, Lowther, Queensberry
1563	**Royal Progress of Queen Mary**		
		Mary	Arrochar Alps, Millfore, Lowthers and Lammermuirs
1645	**Montrose - the Great March**		
		Charles I	Loch Creran,

6

Chronological Summary

		Charles II	Glencoe, Mamores Loch Treig, Glentarf, Glen Roy
1651	**Moncks Campaign**	James VII	Glenshiel, Glen Ling, Strathfarrar, Loch Rannoch, Dalnaspidal
1692	**McGregors, McDonalds & Campbells**	William & Mary	Glen Lyon & Glencoe
1715	**'The Fifteen'**	George I	Ladder Hills, Hills of Mar, Glen Clunie, Loch Lochy, Lairig Leachach, Glen Fyne, Balquhidder
1745	**'The Forty Five'**	George II	Loch Sheil, Loch Moidart, Corrieyairick, Manor & Moffat, Glens Clova, Muick & Dessary
1746	**The Prince in the Heather**	George II	Upper Glen Dessary, Harris, Knoydart, Loch Quoich, Loch Hourn, Glens Sheil, Affric, Cannich
1850	**Queen Victoria at Loch Maree**	Victoria	Lochs Maree, Torridon, Clair and na Oidiche

Looking over Loch Clair to Sgurr Dubh and Sgurr nan Lochan Uaine

The Spread of Christianity in Scotland after the Roman Era

Amongst the books on this subject which I have inspected, I was attracted by the book entitled 'The Celtic Church in Scotland' by Dr. W. Douglas Simpson. In his introduction he remarks that his conclusions are not generally accepted by historians. Be that as it may, I found his development of his theme seemed to fit the evidence, admittedly circumstantial, which is available about this epoch. The maps which I have produced in this connection are largely based on those developed by Dr. Simpson.

Saint Ninian

St. Ninian was probably born about 360 in the British section of Alba, possibly in Cumberland. He was a Christian and a Roman citizen and he decided to go to Rome to be given a monastic training. Although the

The Spread of Christianity in Scotland after the Roman Era

Roman Empire had withdrawn its troops from Alba its church was interested in spreading the Christian faith among the non-Christian peoples left in Alba. On St Ninian's route back to Alba he spent time with the celebrated St.Martin at Tours and remained a fervent disciple of him for the rest of his life. Indeed there are many tangible examples of the relationship with St. Martin in some of the names given to various places and on various Celtic stones at these places on the mission track followed by St. Ninian and his cult followers.

St.Ninian himself started his mission in Whithorn and *Map1* shows sites, bearing his name, in the Pictish portion of the country where there has also been archaeological evidence of Celtic occupation at that time. It is remarkable how closely they follow the line of the military encampments of the Roman legions.

So far as Corbetts and Donalds are concerned Ninian's chapel at Whithorn is close to **the Fleet Hills range of Donalds** which I have associated with him. His cult was probably developed up the east side of the country but there is also evidence of a St. Ninian site in Glen Urquhart in the Great Glen and possibly one in Caithness-shire.

The Saint Ninian Donalds
Cairnsmore of Fleet, Meikle Multaggart, Knee of Cairnsmore

It was amazing to think that nearly 1600 years ago, Saint Ninian from his base in Whithorn could well have been seeing these hills in the same type of thick mist which prevailed when Kenneth and I set out to climb them early in April. We set out from Palnure and proceeded by the old railway viaduct to the old Kennels for Cairnsmore House. We quickly found the pathway which led us directly to the Cairnsmore summit but as we could not see anything we decided that Meikle Multaggart and Knee of Cairnsmore could be left for another day.

The next time we chose a day with a reasonably good forecast We approached the hills from Palnure as I had already done in April and took the good hill-path up to Cairnsmore. Sadly the forecasters were partially wrong and there was thick hill mist at around 2000 feet continuing all the way to the summit. From Cairnsmore we made our way to Meikle Multaggart using the compass and noting the remains of an old fence as we went. This was useful in guiding us back to the summit of Cairnsmore and although the conditions had worsened considerably we continued along the ridge to the large cairn on the Knee of Cairnsmore. As it was also very wet by this time we then cut diagonally across the slope rather than returning along the ridge but found we had chosen a very stony descent.

The Spread of Christianity in Scotland after the Roman Era

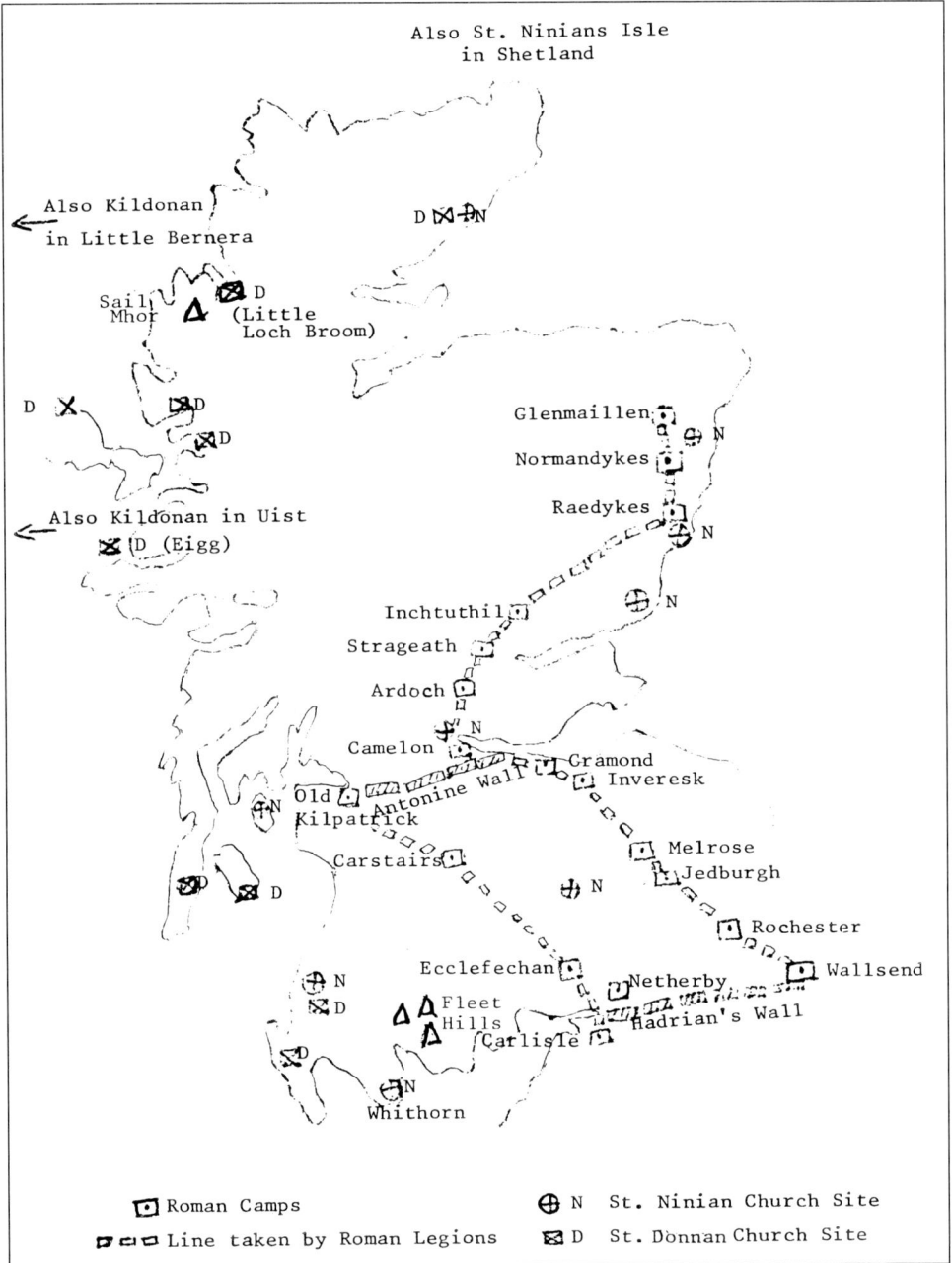

Also St. Ninians Isle
in Shetland

Also Kildonan
in Little Bernera

D ⊠ ⊕N

Sail
Mhor △ ⊠ D
(Little
Loch Broom)

D ✕   ⊠D

⊠D

Glenmaillen
⊕ N
Normandykes

Raedykes
⊕ N

Also Kildonan in Uist
⊠ (D (Eigg)

Inchtuthil
⊕ N
Strageath

Ardoch

⊕ N
Camelon
Cramond
Inveresk

Old ⊕N
Kilpatrick   Antonine Wall

Carstairs

⊕ N   Melrose
Jedburgh

⊠D   Rochester

Ecclefechan   Wallsend
⊕ N   Netherby
⊠ D   Fleet
△ △ Hills   Hadrian's Wall
△   Carlisle
⊠D
⊕N
Whithorn

⊡ Roman Camps   ⊕ N   St. Ninian Church Site

▱▱▱ Line taken by Roman Legions   ⊠ D   St. Donnan Church Site

Map 1: Missions of St. Ninian and St. Donnan

10

The Spread of Christianity in Scotland after the Roman Era

Saint Donnan

In the sixth century, St.Donnan, a contemporary of St. Columba, established himself in the Island of Eigg. After several missions, his martyrdom occurred in Eigg itself in 613. Dedications to St. Donnan and his cult are to be found in Caithness, Wester Ross and the Outer Isles, and in particular at a chapel at Kildonan on Little Loch Broom almost directly opposite to Corbett **Sail Mhor** across the Loch.

Sail Mhor

Saint Donnan must have been able to gaze over the quiet waters of the Loch and contemplate the peace of Sail Mhor. There is now a thriving fish factory at Ardessie and Saint Donnan's peaceful contemplations would not be so easy to obtain.

We set off up Allt Airdeasaidh near a small electricity sub- station and continued up south-west on relatively easy going. The final part of the climb, just before the summit, was however very steep and tiring. The weather was superb and we were very happy to be able to relax in the sunshine on the top enjoying the magnificent views of the Lochs and of the Summer Isles. Ben Mor Coigach, impressive and attractive as ever, precluded us from seeing the Lochinver Hills. It was interesting too, to pick out the road system on the peninsula between the two estuaries with Beinn Ghobhlach in command. But the magnificent An Teallach range enthralled us and I could relive the splendid scramble which I had over the pinnacles there.

We decided to descend in a south easterly direction as the slopes looked easier. But we did not, as we had hoped, avoid a steep descent which would have been difficult in wet and misty conditions. We then turned due east to the junction of the first tributary with the Allt Airdeasaidh as we thought we could see a path down the far side of the stream. However we found that we could not cross the stream and had to make do with a reasonably good deer track which took us most of the way back to the road.

Saint Columba

About this time, in 563, St. Columba, who is historically the great Christian leader in Scotland, set up his monastery in Iona. Adamnan, ninth Abbot of Iona, and a great Christian leader in his own right, is the most important biographer of Columba. Columba was a member of the Irish royal family, as indeed was Adamnan, and had access to the royal families of the Britons, the Scots and the Picts. Indeed he had an important influence on the selection of the Dalriadan king. The Picts were not on friendly terms with the Dalriadans who were regarded as intruders. Thus, although Columba , with his royal connections, established relations with Kings of the Picts and also

The Spread of Christianity in Scotland after the Roman Era

Kings of the Britons, Adamnan does not record any monasteries established in these areas. He does, however, record Columba's visits to these royal courts, all probably in the northern section of Pictland as it then was. His main pilgrimages were around the Firth of Lorn, the Sound of Mull, Iona and Tiree. Although Columba had made contact with Bridei, King of the Picts, and seemed to have a good relationship with him, the main breakthroughs into the heart of Pictland were the missions of St. Moluag in 592 and of St. Maelrubha in 673.

Saint Moluag

St. Moluag based his mission on the Island of Lismore. One of his missions was in an easterly direction and ended up in the area of Keith where about a century later he was followed by St. Maelrubha.

Saint Maelrubha

St. Maelrubha was, like Columba, a member of the Irish royal family but seems to have had the considerable asset of having a Pictish mother possibly making him more acceptable to the Pictish people. He based his mission in Applecross in the shadow of the grim Corbetts, **Beinn Bhan** and **Sgurr a' Chaorachain**. (*Map 2*)

From Applecross he seems to have made several missions. One was to Skye where he was ferried over from a place called Aiseag near Kyle of Lochalsh. One of his churches in Skye was at Elgol, near Bonnie Prince Charlie's cave and possibly near Kilmarie.

His northern missionary effort is more interesting. Most probably he went from Applecross to Loch Carron where a Maelrubha chapel is to be found. From Loch Carron he would have proceeded to Loch Maree (Maelrubha's loch). To get there I speculate that he would have used the shortest cross country route into Glen Torridon, namely that by Lochs Coulin and Clair passing Corbetts **Sgurr Dubh** and **Sgorr nan Lochain Uaine** on his left. He would then have continued into Glen Docherty by Kinlochewe and on to Loch Maree. At Loch Maree he established a chapel on Eilean Ma Rui looking onto Corbetts **Beinn Airigh Charr** and **Beinn Lair**. From here he would have continued to Lairg by a route not established. It is likely that Saint Maelrubha would have kept away from the coast because of the danger of Viking raiders around there. I have therefore made a speculation that he crossed to the north side of Loch Maree and proceeded across the tracks of the Great Wilderness by Carnmore passing Corbetts **Beinn a'Chaisgean Mor, Beinn Dearg Mhor and Beinn Dearg Bheag** and through to Dundonnell. From here, again avoiding the coastal regions, he could well have proceeded by Braemore and Loch Glascarnoch and Loch Vaich up to Deanich Lodge. This latter speculation may be supported to some extent by a reference by Dr. A. B. Scott in his description of Saint Maelrubha's northern mission to the formation of a foundation at Easter Carron. This probably refers to the Strath Carron near Glen Calvie Lodge and Corbett **Carn Chuinneag**. This is on the way to Lairg where he founded a chapel. He finally got up to Farr on the north coast. Some reports state that he was killed there in a Viking raid while other reports refer to his death in Applecross.

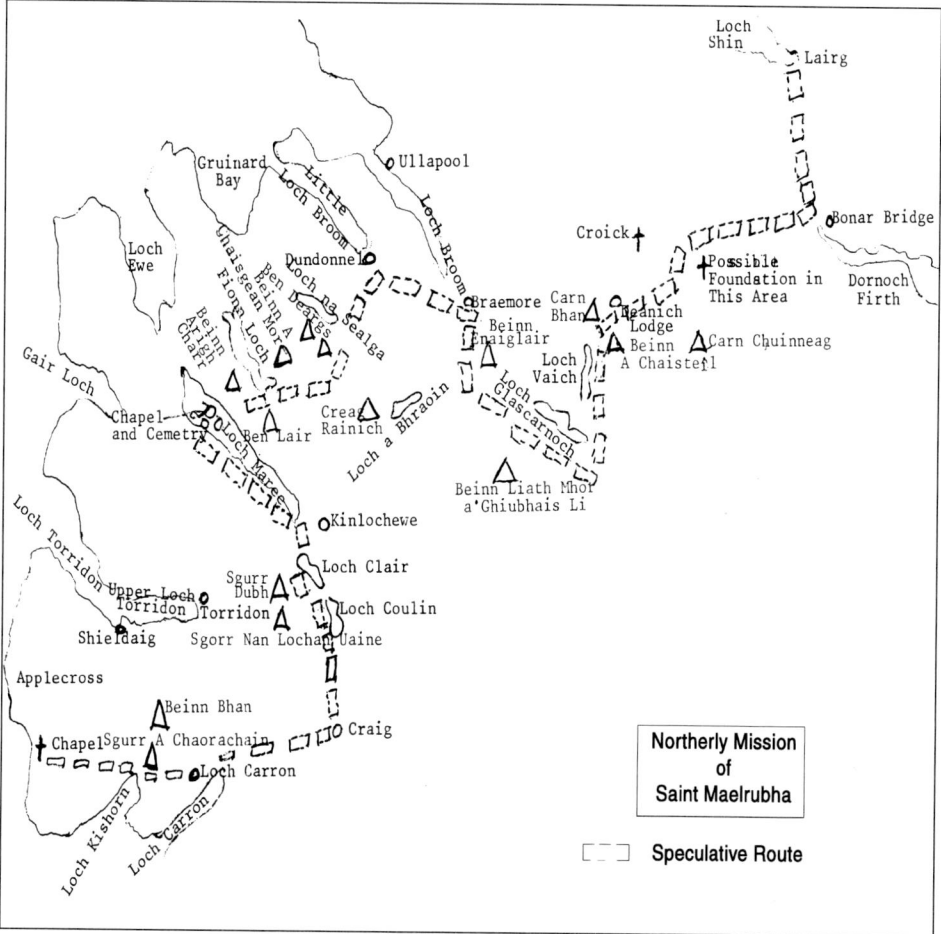

Map 2

Saint Maelrubha's Corbetts
The Applecross Corbetts – Beinn Bhan and Sgurr a'Chaorachain

Since Saint Maelrubha had based himself in Applecross, it was natural to start with the Applecross Corbetts themselves. I had been several times to my friends at Loch Carron with a view to climbing these two but had always refrained because of bad weather. I wanted a good day for them if possible.

Having heard a good forecast for the next day, Munro and I therefore decided to drive from Edinburgh leaving in the evening spending the night at Loch Carron. The plan was successful as, although it was overcast when we left Loch Carron, we reached the summit of Bealach na Bo to find Sgurr a'Chaorachain clear of cloud and Beinn Bhan rapidly clearing. It was, however, bitterly cold and without delay, leaving the car at the car park, we walked up the track to the TV aerial. From there it was a marvellous walk out to the summit of Sgurr a Chaorachain. There was only one slight piece of scrambling where my young dog Tom had to be lifted down. In good spirits although still very cold, we set off for Beinn Bhan skirting the TV aerial summit and avoiding the 'dog bad-step'. We reached the bealach above Coire nan Cuileag from where we contoured round a ledge to reach Bealach nan Arr which is marked by a cairn. From here we found an extremely well cairned path among the rocks going up the east side of the ridge. This led to the summit plateau. From there, it was simple to continue over the rocky ground to the summit of Beinn Bhan, although the line of cairns ceased on the plateau with the summit cairn in sight. We ought to have taken a bearing from the last cairn to the summit but in the clear conditions, we did not anticipate any problem in finding the cairned route again to descend through the rocks. Despite the strong cold wind we spent some time admiring the panoramic view from Beinn Bhan. The Cuillins, just clear of mist, Raasay and Skye, the Five Sisters with Beinn Sgritheall in the background and the dim shapes of the Knoydart hills, the Glen Affric hills particularly the Mam Sodhail group, the Fannichs, the Deargs, and the three Torridon giants along with An Teallach and some of the Wilderness tops made an unforgettable view. The Loch Carron and Achnashellach hills were specially fine silhouetted against the hazy sun. Reluctantly but coldly we left the summit and looked for our cairned path but among the great sea of stones we just could not pick it up. We set off hopefully but could see no signs of it until we noticed that my dog Tom was trotting away down the hill to our right .We decided to follow him and sure enough he led us to the cairned ascent we had used on the way up. Not a method of route finding to be recommended. We soon reached the Bealach nan Arr and from there decided to try to pick up a track shown on my map contouring round the Coire nan Cuileag to the main road. But we failed to find it and had to make our way to the road over some rough boggy ground. The splendid day was completed by superb views as we descended the Bealach na Bo pass to Loch Kishorn.

Sgurr Dubh and Sgorr nan Lochan Uaine

On one of the days I was at Loch Carron with a view to climbing the Applecross Corbetts it was very wet and misty over the loch and I thought I might as well drive round to the Loch Clair and Loch Coulin hills in the hope of improving weather. When I reached Loch Clair the sun was shining. I walked along this most beautiful road with the hills I was planning to climb showing through the trees round the Loch. I came across a young stalker at work in his shed who kindly directed me to an excellent stalker's path following the Allt na Luib right up into Coire an Leth -Uillt (where there is a small stone stalker's shelter). I continued onto the ridge amid intermittent showers of rain and hail accompanied by a gale force wind. The last slopes of Sgorr an Lochan Uaine are very stony and in the fierce wind I had to use my hands to keep my balance. There were rewarding views of the magnificent hills to the north and also I could see the rough and stony ridge I would be following to Sgurr Dubh, interspersed with numerous small lochans. Because of the stony nature of the ground and the strong wind the ridge could not be rushed and it took longer than I expected to reach the summit cairn on Sgurr Dubh. I descended steeply and slowly to the Allt na Luib path between the trees. This is a very photogenic area and the views of Beinn Eighe and Liathach as I returned to the car were every bit as good as the picture postcards show them to be.

Beinn Dearg Mhor, Beinn Dearg Bheag and Beinn a'Chaisgean Mor, Beinn Airigh Charr and Beinn Lair

The track from Carnmore on the way to Dundonnel passes the first three Corbetts and my 'speculative saintly route' takes in what is one of the finest of all the Corbetts in my opinion, namely Beinn Dearg Mhor.

To tackle this group and also Beinn Airigh Charr and Beinn Lair, we parked our car at Kernsary and walked over the rough ground to Carnmore. We had a look round the lodge, the gillies' bothy (both of which were securely locked) and the outhouses. One of the latter could have been used in a dire emergency but it was quite filthy. We pitched our tents and awoke the following morning to a glorious day of sunshine.

We set out up the Allt Bruthach an Easain rising from about 600 feet at Carnmore to about 1500 feet at Loch Beinn Dearg. Here we traversed along the south side of Beinn Dearg Mor to the bealach below Beinn Dearg Bheag and from there comfortably reached the summit a further 500 feet

Sgurr na Laocainn and the slopes of Beinn a'Chaisgean Mor from Carnmore

up. We could not believe our luck to find the Great Wilderness views so clear. After a period of contemplation at the top we proceeded to the magnificent Beinn Dearg Mhor, a further 1000 feet of climbing approximately. The ridge was a fine one indeed and after a further period of contemplation at the summit, we decided to make a steep descent to Loch Beinn Dearg. From the Loch a climb of about 700 feet was required to get us back to Lochan Feith Mhic-illean. The ascent to Beinn a Chaisgean Mor was rather humdrum after the Beinn Dearg Mhor ridge but it took us directly to the top. From here we made another steep descent -involving some scrambling- down the gully between Beinn a'Chaisgean Mor and Sgurr na Laocainn. This as we had planned brought us out directly at our tents.

It must be rare to have such clarity of views and all day long the views in all directions were fascinating. The tips of Ben Hope and, we thought, Ben Klibreck were visible in the far distance, the Outer Hebrides, Skye and the Cuillins, the Suilven group and Beinn Mor Assynt, the Beinn Dearg group, the Fannichs, the Beinn Eighe group, Beinn Lair and Beinn Airigh Charr gave us a superb day of picking out hills we knew and had climbed. Needless to say the monarch of them all was regal An Teallach.

Carn Ban and Beinn a'Chaisteal

Hugh and I spent the night at Garve en route to a trip round the north coast. From Garve we intended to climb Carn Ban and also Beinn a Chaisteal. We drove up the road from Black Bridge and after collecting the key from the keeper continued up the rough road to Gleann Beag. We crossed the bridge over the Allt Bheargais and followed an excellent stalker's track up the escarpment to the moorland above. We had no trouble crossing this rather tussocky ground and soon reached the summit of Carn Ban. The superb views from the summit covered Bens Hope, Loyal and Klibreck, Morven in Caithness, the Foinaven group, the Ben Dearg group, Ben Wyvis, the Fannichs, An Teallach, the Strath Farrar hills and Carn Chuinneag and our objective on the return journey down the glen, Beinn a'Chaisteal. On the road down the glen we left the car at the highest part of the road under Beinn a'Chaisteal which we easily climbed in under two hours.

Carn Chuinneag

We approached this hill from Ardgay and took the road up Strath Carron (where as mentioned above, there is possibly some evidence of Saint Maelrubha's mission to this area) and passed The Craigs in error. We found ourselves at Croik Church where the names of all those evicted from the glen in favour of sheep are inscribed on a window.

We returned to the bridge at The Craigs and drove up to Glen Calvie where we found that the keeper had a copy of our letter of permission from the estate agent in his hand and was expecting us. We then drove up the beautiful Glen Calvie to the junction with the Diebidale Lodge track where we left the car. A stalker's path leads from here onto the hill and was one of the best of its kind I have been on. We followed this track up to the summit ridge where it makes a T-junction with a track coming up the face of the hill. A continuation to the east soon saw us at the small bealach to the west of the summit and the top was quickly reached from there.

The Eventual Establishment of the Christian Church in Scotland

It was not until the time of Kenneth MacAlpin that the Scotic church of St. Columba began to establish itself in the areas formerly Pictland. The influence of his church then spread throughout the combined peoples of Dalriada and Pictland. But, in the seventh century , the Angles of Northumbria were extending their military influence across into the British area of Strathclyde. The Angles were still pagan in their religious beliefs at this stage but St. Aidan of Iona in 612 managed to convert them to Christianity although there was also a mission sponsored from Rome. At this time, the Roman and the Celtic churches had some differences in their theological beliefs and the famous Synod of Whitby took place in 664 when the Roman ideas prevailed. The Celtic church effectively withdrew, and the four Scottish peoples eventually shared a common Christian religious faith in the majority of their territories.

Murray with Mount Battock on the horizon

The Unification of Scotland

The various Roman attempts to subdue Scotland never completely succeeded. Agricola, Antoninus and Severus conducted campaigns defeating the Scottish in battle but never subjugating them totally. The people I have called Scottish were at that time comprised of a variety of what were really large tribal groups; the Picts, Angles, Britons, Scots, Galwegians and Norsemen.

The history of the Picts is difficult to disentangle.They were first referred to by Roman writers in the third century and Bede in the sixth century refers to the southern Picts and the northern Picts and to the influence of Ninian on the Southern Picts. There is evidence too that the Picts had a substantial navy which was able to conduct operations against the Romans. Concurrently with the development of the Pictish nation was the development of Dalriada and the Scots, Strathclyde and the Britons and Northumbria and the Angles. The Norsemen too had a strong hold on the northern tip of the Scottish mainland and also controlled the Outer Isles and the Orkneys and Shetlands. The detailed history of this amalgam of peoples is not straightforward and the emergence of Scotland as we now know it took many centuries. Several of the battles between these warring groups were of importance, as, if the result had been different, the unification of Scotland would itself have followed a different course.

Battle of Nechtansmere

The first battle to which I refer is the Battle of Nechtansmere in 685. (*Map 3)* Midway through the seventh century, the Northumbrians, having defeated the Mercians to the south, turned their attention to northward expansion. The King of Northumbria, Ecgfrith, marched north and massacred the Pictish army under its King Bridei, in 672. But Bridei survived and rallied the Picts. Ecgfrith raised another army and again marched against the Picts. This time Bridei was ready and at Dunnichen Moss he inflicted a resounding defeat on Ecgfrith who was killed in the action, the Battle of Nechtansmere. The Angles were forced back through Stirling and West Lothian. As a result of this battle the incursion of the Angles into Northern Britain was decisively halted for many years.

Mount Battock

It was with the Pictish background in my mind that I visited my friends Jim and Janet Cosgrove in Letham, Angus. It had been to a large extent due to Jim's enthusiasm that the historical importance of the Battle of Nechtansmere in 685 was recognised in 1985 by the erection of a memorial commemorating the 1300th anniversary of the battle.

On the day in June when we decided to tackle **Mount Battock**, the Corbett which I was allocating to the Pictish area, we drove up Glen Esk to Millden Lodge. The Glen was looking beautiful in the morning sunshine after a sudden heavy snowfall. We parked the car at the lodge and set off up the west side of the Burn of Turret. Shortly after emerging from the woods we crossed the burn where my old map had indicated a ford. Happily there was now a bridge whence a bulldozed road leads to the summit of the Hill of Fingray. We continued along the ridge - part of the border between Kincardine and Angus - over the Hill of Saughs until a final climb landed us on the summit of Mount Battock not too far from the triple border intersection of the above two counties and Aberdeenshire. There was evidence of much wild life with the bird songs exceptionally fine; we saw many types of birds – curlew, buzzard,

The Unification of Scotland

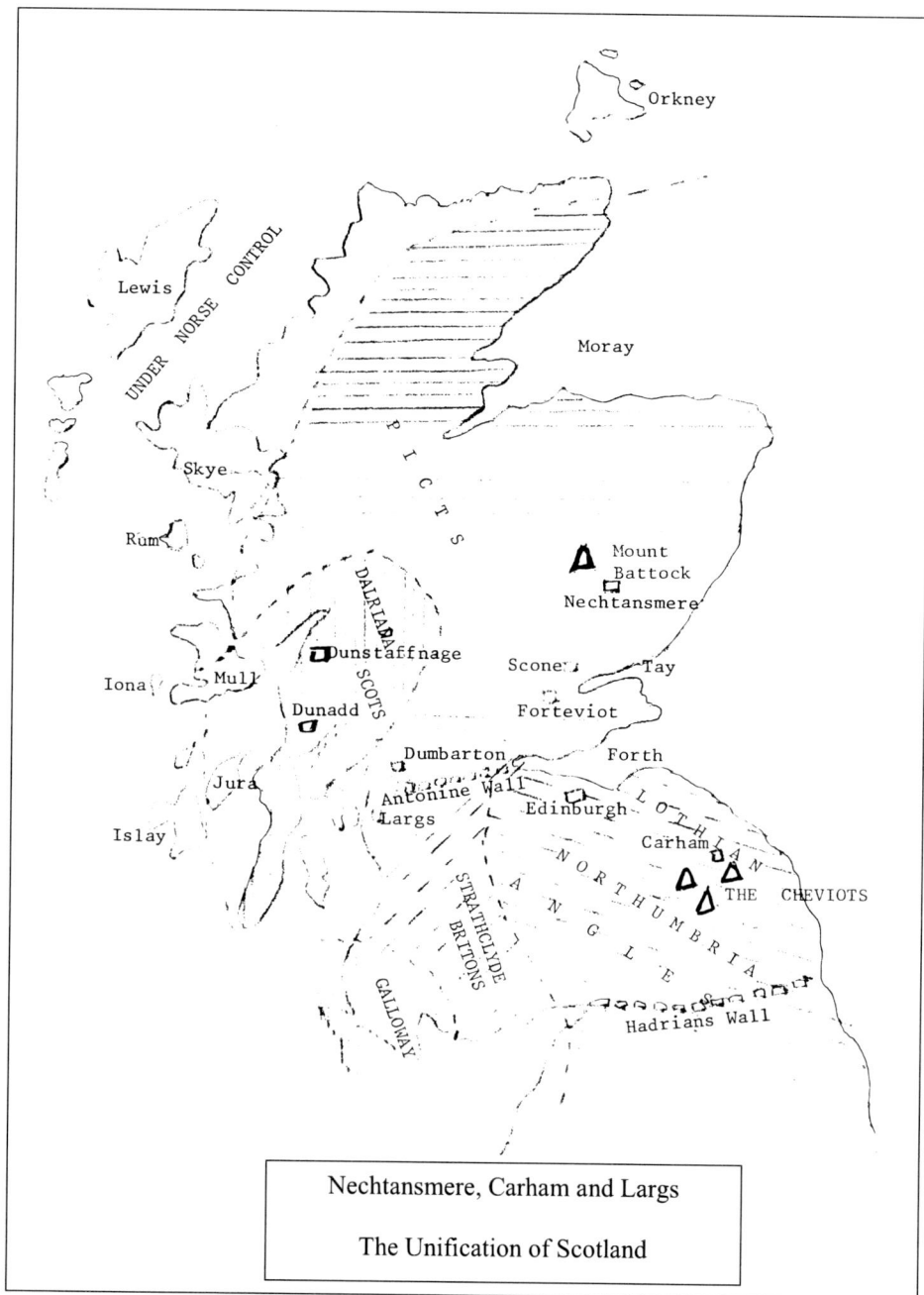

Orkney

Lewis

UNDER NORSE CONTROL

Moray

Skye

P I C T S

Rum

DALRIADA

Mount
Battock
Nechtansmere

Iona   Mull   Dunstaffnage   Scone   Tay

SCOTS

Dunadd   Forteviot

Dumbarton   Forth

Jura   Antonine Wall   Edinburgh   L O T H I A N

Largs   Carham

Islay   N O R T H U M B R I A   THE CHEVIOTS

A N G L E

STRATHCLYDE BRITONS

GALLOWAY   Hadrians Wall

Nechtansmere, Carham and Largs

The Unification of Scotland

Map 3

21

lapwing, oyster-catcher, plover, peregrine and many smaller birds. There were numerous rabbits, squirrels, hares and plenty red deer. We descended by the slopes of Bennygray and Mount Een stopping for a chat with the stalker.

Kenneth mac Alpin

The next significant step in the emergence of the kingdom of Scotland was the Kingship of Kenneth mac Alpin over Scots and Picts, in 841. Kenneth is often referred to as the first king of both peoples but this is not so and there are several cases before him where there was a joint king of both peoples. His kingship included the title of King of Picts and it was not until his grandson Donald II that the King was referred to as the King of Alba. The dynasty of Kenneth effectively lasted till the accession of Macbeth in 1040. Macbeth reigned successfully for 17 years when Malcolm Canmore defeated and slew both Macbeth and Macbeth's successor, Lulach, thereby starting the Malcolm Canmore dynasty.

Battle of Carham

After the Battle of Nechtansmere in 685, the Picts controlled the area probably down to the Forth, but control of the country south of the Forth – Clyde line down into Bernicia was in dispute. The Northumbrian kings had for some time been much involved in battles with the Danes. While they were so occupied, the Scots, as mentioned above, had been amalgamated with the Picts and were able to consolidate strongly their hold on the area down to the Forth. In 973, the English king, Edgar and the Scottish king, Kenneth II, met at Chester. Edgar ceded to Scotland the control of the Lothians – a recognition which was, in fact, of a position which already existed. The control of Bernicia, approximately Northumberland and Durham in today's terms, was certainly more open to doubt and continued to be a matter of contention after the Chester meeting. It was possibly over this issue and not the control of the Lothians that the battle of Carham was fought in 1018. It appears from such contemporary records which are available that this was a resounding victory for the Scots. Malcolm II may well have succeeded in winning the overlordship of the Bernicians for some time as a result of this victory but whether that was the case or not, the victory at Carham reinforced Scottish domination of the area between the Tweed and the Forth.

The Cheviots

The village of Carham is quite close to my birthplace, Kelso, and this area is associated for me with the hills of the area, the Cheviots – the hills of my youth. I still recall with satisfaction when at the age of ten I reached the top of Staerough when I was on holiday at Yetholm with my grand-aunt. Her house was appropriately named Staerough View.

After reference to the map I can usually recall the features of any particular hill climb but, as for any hillwalker, there are certain hill-walks which are preeminent. For me, such ones are my first and last hills among the Munros, the Corbetts and the Donalds, the Inaccessible Pinnacle, the Ben Nevis cliffs, the Rhum Cuillins, the An Teallach ridge, Ben Lomond and the Five Sisters of Kintail. But the first hill-walk of all is never forgotten and my earliest walks were in the Cheviots – over 70 years ago. The first was the ascent of Staerough, - a small Cheviot outlier near Yetholm, as I have already mentioned (*Map 4*). Shortly afterwards came my first ascent of Cheviot itself, organised by an enterprising school teacher for his class. It remains clearly in my memory as it was quite an adventure for us at that time. It involved cycling from Kelso to Yetholm, uphill all the way, and then following the Bowmont valley past Primside Mill and Mowhaugh farms up to Sourhope farm -the end of the road. We were started off with a stimulating marching tune on the pipes - the piper becoming a Professor of Theology in later life - as we walked up the path from Sourhope farm. We had sunshine all the way up the ridge along side the Dodd burn and up through the Hen Hole to our sandwich stop at Auchope Cairn now classified as a Donald. I still recall the feeling of disappointment at the summit of Cheviot itself; it was just an old pole surrounded by a huge morass of glutinous peat. Nowadays it is an Ordnance Survey pillar but still surrounded by a morass of glutinous peat. However we felt a great sense of achievement and it was a happy group who cycled in the evening sun down the Bowmont valley and then down the hill from Yetholm to Kelso. Little did I know then that I had ascended my first 'Donald'.

Windy Gyle

The Edinburgh Glen More walking club had a June outing to the Cheviots including Windy Gyle in the walk. Cars were parked at Cocklawfoot farm. Passing Kelsocleuch farm en route, a good path along Kelsocleuch rig took us comfortably to the Windy Gyle summit, the farthest west of the Cheviot group of Donalds. The visibility was reasonably good and the Scottish border land with all its happy memories claimed my attention as we walked along the rather eroded path which is now part of the Pennine Way. The Eildons, Ruberslaw near Hawick, the Penielheugh memorial, Hume Castle and my first hill, the humdrum little Staerough, could all be picked out. The walk continued to Auchope Cairn but the muddy track to the Cheviot summit did not appeal to me nor to any others of the party. A good path led down the side of the Cheviot burn to the cars.

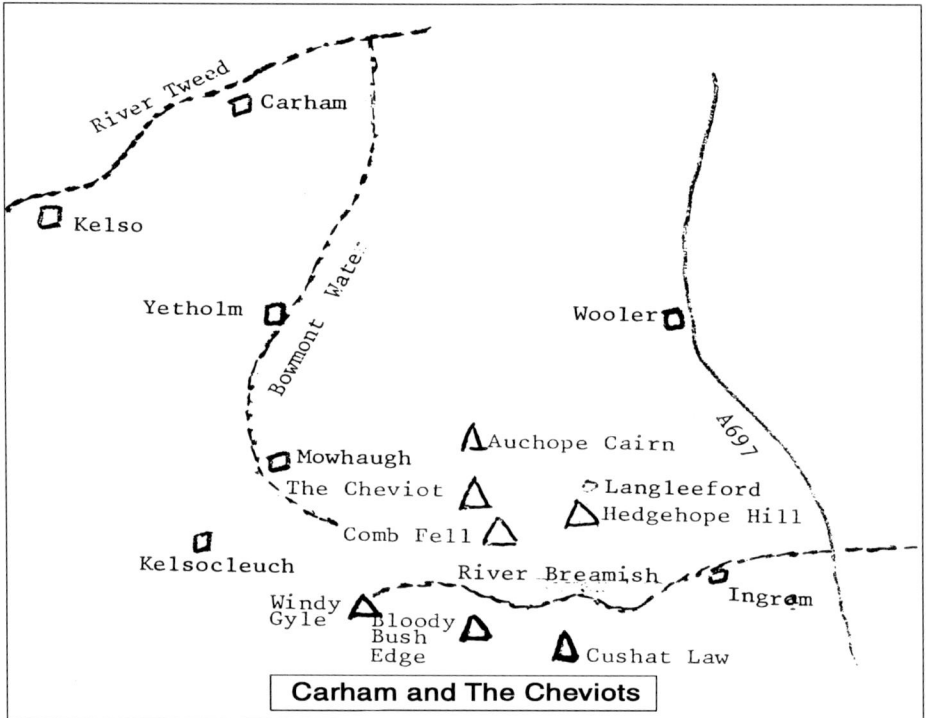

Map 4

The English Cheviot Donalds

For the English Cheviot Donalds, probably crossed by the Scottish forces involved in the Battle of Otterburn in 1388, Murray and I stayed at a very comfortable farmhouse, Greenside Hill, up the Breamish valley south of Wooler. It was a lovely summer's day when we set off on what for me at least was a fairly ambitious day's walk. It involved about 18 miles and 4500 feet of climbing. The car was parked at the Hawsey Burn car park in the Harthope valley and a good path then took us over the shoulder of Broadhope Hill. This came to a farm fence which could then be followed to Scauld Hill. From here the path turned west to lead to the bleak summit of Cheviot. In light mist we proceeded to Cairn Hill and, via Scotsman's Knowe at the head of the Breamish Valley - along a rough track at the edge of some recent forestry. This crossed the track leading to Uswayford and continued uphill to Bloody Bush Edge where we turned. We retraced our steps for a short distance and then cut the corner to ascend Coldlaw Cairn and follow the fence along the top of Comb Fell ridge and on to the top of Hedgehope Hill. A steep descent led to the

The Unification of Scotland

Long Crags and down to a good bridge over the Harthope Burn back to the car. It was interesting to check our speed. The walk took us eight and three quarter hours and included a good proportion of rough and wet going. I was up to my thigh in one mud hole.

Next morning we left Greenside Hill farm to climb Cushat Law and parked the car at Hartside. A sign marked 'Permissive Path' induced us, rather stupidly, to take a direction over Het Hill parallel exactly to the one we wanted over Scaud Knowe. We reached Shank House where we joined the 'Salters Road'. This led to the 1600 foot bealach below Bush Knowe and a rough track easily led to Cushat Law. The views were splendid. The cairn at Bloody Bush Edge and the one at Windy Gyle were nearly in line. In the sunshine the clarity of the Cheviot ridge and summit, Cairn Hill, Coldlaw Cairn, Comb Fell and Hedgehope Hill enabled us to appreciate the walk we had done the previous day. We cut down north east to rejoin the 'Salter's Road' and on to the road at Low Bleakhope. We stopped to chat to the farmer and to compliment him on the fine showing of his garden-not too often a feature of hill farms. Along with his son at High Bleakhope farm, they had 2000 sheep, mostly Cheviots crossed with Swaledales, on the hills. The Breamish valley gave us a very pleasant walk back to our car to finish our Cheviot outing.

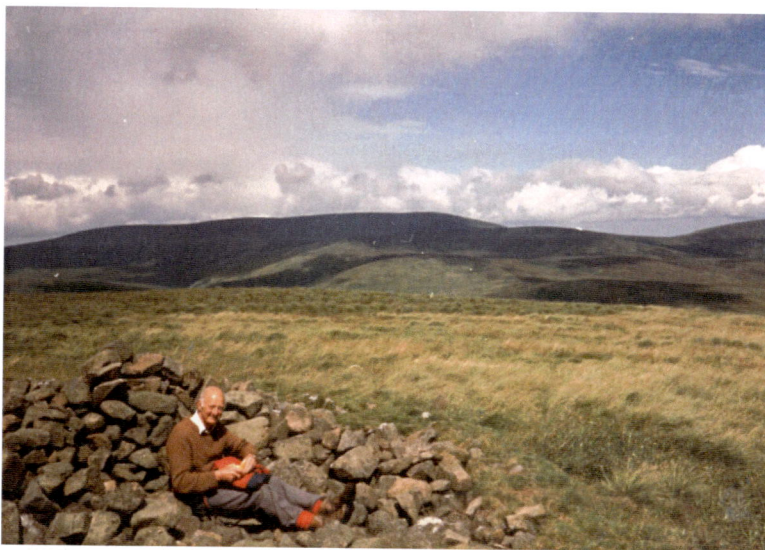

The Cheviots – Bloody Bush Edge and Cushat Law from Cairn Hill

The Unification of Scotland

Strathclyde and Galloway

Malcolm II controlled the Scots, the Picts, and the Angles, certainly down to the Tweed. He was succeeded by his grandson, Duncan I, (the 'Duncan' of Shakespeare) then King of Strathclyde, who incorporated Strathclyde into his enlarged kingdom. This completed another stage in the unification of Scotland. Duncan I was, of course, succeeded by Macbeth.

In the mid ninth century the Galloway tribes supported Kenneth mac Alpin in his amalgamation of the Scots and the Picts. Kenneth remained on friendly terms with the Galloway tribes and indeed gave one of his daughters in marriage to a Galloway tribal chieftain. In the time of Macbeth, a famous Norse, Jarl Thorfinn, ruled over Galloway as parts of mainland Scotland. Macbeth and Thorfinn, possibly cousins, could well have been on friendly terms. Macbeth was killed in battle in 1057 by Malcolm Canmore (son of the 'Shakespearean murdered' Duncan I) and Jarl Thorfinn is thought to have died about the same time. Malcolm Canmore married his widow, Ingibiorg. As a result Galloway was for the first time brought under the Scottish king's control.

There remained unconsolidated only the areas still under the influence of the Norwegian king. The Battle of Largs, discussed later in King Haakon's Expedition, was the beginning of the completion of unification.

Strathclyde
The Rhinns of Kells

A long ridge, the Rhinns of Kells, (*Map 5*) running almost north to south from Loch Doon to Loch Dee is situated on the western side of the Strathclyde of olden times. Although there are no specific major historical events associated with this ridge, there must have been almost constant warlike activity between the Angles to the East and the Britons to the west.

At the north end the ridge separates the sources of the Dee and the Doon on the west side from the sources of the Deugh and the Ken on the east. Loch Doon is close to the north beginning of the long ridge and at the south end Loch Dee and Clatteringshaws Loch are located. The ridge is a splendid one and, if possible, it deserves to be walked all in one day . This was most conveniently done for me using a car at each end of the ridge. It is a really commanding ridge about twelve miles in length and for about three-quarters of its length it is over two thousand feet.

We left one car at the farm of Clenrie, with the shepherd's permission. We then drove to the Garryhorn road end where, to our consternation, we found that there was a locked gate on the road up to the lead mines. We were just parking the car and putting on our boots when the farmer, Mr Wallace, to whom I had written in advance for permission to go on up to the mines,

The Unification of Scotland

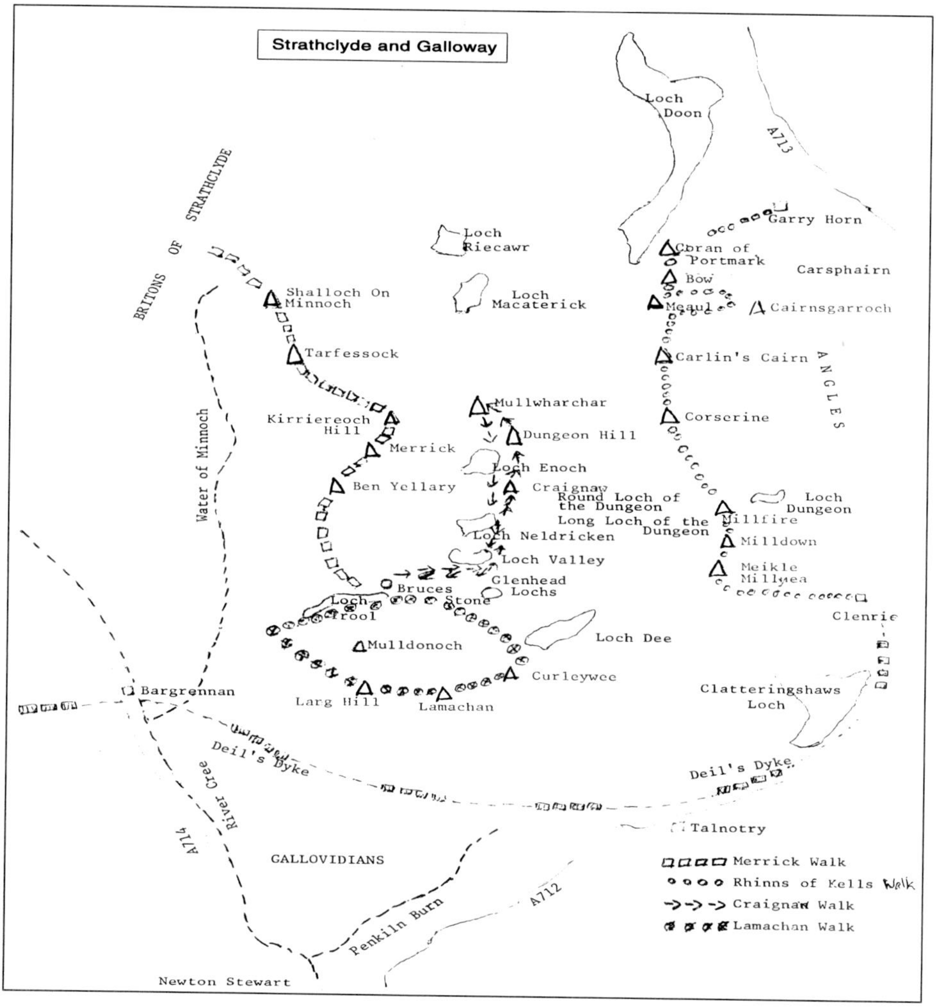

Map 5

The Unification of Scotland

Jim and Tom on the Rhinns of Kells looking over the Silver Strand

appeared and opened the gate for us. He assured us that he would be around to open it for us to get out when we returned at night. We then drove the car well up into the interesting old miner's village and mines and found the wicket gate in the wall mentioned in the Southern Uplands Guide Book. But we could not find much of a path and had to take a compass bearing to be sure that it was Coran of Portmark that we were climbing. We then walked over the three little tops of Bow and went on to Meaul. Here we left our rucksacks at the cairn and walked out to Cairnsgarroch and back. We then proceeded by Goat Craigs to Carlins Cairn with its massive and unexplained cairn. Reputedly it was erected by a widow who had helped Robert the Bruce and he had given her the land when he became king. The main summit of the ridge is Corserine, which, when I climbed it, was both a Corbett and a Donald. As we walked along the ridge at this point the views over the Silver Strand to Craignaw and Dungeon Hill and indeed to the Merrick range further west were really superb. It was amazing too, that the hills of Arran could be picked up and also Ailsa Craig. We left the cairn at Corserine and soon met the path coming up from Backhill of the Bush over to the Polharrow Burn. Down below we could see the Round Loch of the Dungeon and the Long Loch of the Dungeon and the treacherous nature of the Silver Strand was clearly visible. An enjoyable walk took us along the ridge over Millfire Milldown to Meikle Millyea. As the true top is actually south of the cairn and Ordnance Survey pillar we left our rucksacks at the cairn and walked across to the true top. On returning to the cairn we cut off by the Rocking Stone ridge and then south east to Clenrie. We had a long chat with the shepherd and his wife and then drove back to Garryhorn where Mr. Wallace was kindly around to open the locked gate. After expressing our appreciation and having a chat with Mr. Wallace and his wife, a really enjoyable day's walk was rounded off with a meal in Carsphairn.

Galloway
Craignaw, Dungeon Hill and Mullwharcher

Although I have not found any major historical incident to associate with these Donalds it seems probable that Robert the Bruce may have sheltered in this area in the early stages of his campaign against Edward I of England. As Rev. C. H. Dick mentions in his book, 'The Highways and Byways of Galloway', the place names around these hills all suggest forestry; Backhill of the Bush, Tarfessock – a shaggy or bushy hill, the Saugh Burn – the burn of the willows, the Pulskaig Burn - the burn of the hawthorn trees and so on. It would be an appropriate area for the incident when Bruce's small party was split up and he was trailed by a bloodhound. He managed to kill the dog and obtained shelter from a farmer's widow. Could she have been the lady of Carlins Craig? Shortly after this episode he regrouped and successfully defeated an English contingent at the skirmish of Moss Raploch.

Frances, Munro and I left Newton Stewart and parked the car at Bruce's Stone in Glen Trool. We took the path up to the Gairland Burn to Loch Valley. The track was very wet underfoot and it took us over an hour to reach the stepping stones over the Mid Burn. As one ascends the rough path up the Gairland Burn, a cairn can be picked up behind a wall on the side of the Mid Burn and it is here that the stepping stones are located. We had no difficulty in crossing dry shod. We then continued north east up the slopes of Craignaw – very rough going indeed with no sign of a path and reached the summit of Craignaw in two and a quarter hours. After enjoying the magnificent views of the Merrick range, the Rhinns of Kells, the Minigaff hills, the Fleet hills and the hills around Ayr (with possibly Ailsa Craig just visible), we continued to Dungeon Hill taking a bearing slightly north of west, until we found a suitable gully to get through the rocks circling Craignaw to the north. Fortunately the visibility remained good and we could see our way down an extremely grassy slope which was rather slippery in the wet conditions. We spotted the cairn in the bealach and from there we ascended the south west end of Dungeon Hill and reached its summit cairn in one and three quarter hours from Craignaw. The view from here was just as good and we remarked on the large number of lochs which we had seen; Loch Valley, Loch Neldricken, Loch Arron, Dry Loch, Round Loch of the Dungeon, Loch Long of the Dungeon, Loch Dee, Clatteringshaws Loch and Loch Enoch. Later we saw Loch Riecawr, Loch Macaterick and Loch Doon from Mullwharcher. At the cairn we descended to cross the Pulskaig Burn, fortunately not in spate, and again experienced very rough territory in ascending Mullwharcher.

Mullwharcher from the Devil's Bowling Green

We had by now been going for five and a half hours and, in view of the rough going we had experienced, we considered whether it would be a good idea to continue round Loch Enoch and return over Merrick. The thought of a further 1000feet of climbing on Merrick, the crossing of the Elgin Lane, the possibly rough going before getting there and also a suspicion that the weather was changing for the worse made us decide to return along the east side of Loch Enoch. We took the opportunity to walk on the famous white sands; at one time they were laboriously carried down for use in sharpening and grinding. We then ascended the Craig Neldricken ridge aiming for Loch Arron to get past the continuation of the Dungeon Hill rocks. Our forecast of a change in the weather was correct as we were suddenly hit by a most severe hailstorm and strong wind which forced us to stop and put on all our spare clothes and turn our backs to the wind as the wind and hail on our faces was really painful. The storm lasted for about a quarter of an hour and passed over leaving us in thick mist and for the first time that day we had to use our compasses to strike the end of Loch Neldricken near the Murder Hole. From here we climbed up the ridge taking us down into the Gairland Burn valley. We reached the car in about nine hours from leaving. I thought that this walk was the toughest of the Donalds and a lot tougher than many a Munro or Corbett.

Ardgour – Loch nan Gabhar and Beinn na h'Uamha

Somerled and the Norsemen

Morvern, Ardgour, Sunart, Moidart and The Isles

The areas of Morvern, Ardgour, Sunart, Moidart and indeed the Hebridean Islands are specifically linked with the great warrior chief, Somerled and his successors. They contain some of the most superb hills and the Corbetts among them, particularly the islands group, often involve individual expeditions. Somerled's influence on the development of Scotland is probably not so well recognised as it deserves but to him must be given the credit of starting off the final stage of the unification of the country we now know as Scotland.

It was Somerled, who, around 1130, took on the fierce Norsemen in battle and evicted them from the West Scottish mainland and continued to battle with them until he controlled all the Hebrides. Not only was that to his credit, but he also founded a dynasty, The Lordship of the Isles, which influenced Scottish history for over four hundred years. Indeed, through the female line it was a progenitor of the Stewart Kings of Scotland and later Britain.

The first historical records about Somerled arise in Morvern. He is reputed to have returned there with his father from Ireland and to have been invited by the local clan, the McInnes clan, to lead them in attacking the

32

invading Norsemen. The precise location of the fighting which took place is not known but it may well have been close to Ardtornish, a place which was associated with many future activities of the Somerled dynasty. In this first recorded battle Somerled seems to have shown great skill and leadership and he succeeded in evicting the Norsemen from Morvern. Nigel Tranter's novel, 'The Lord of the Isles' gives a graphic description of the battle, probably not far removed from historical accuracy. The splendid Corbetts **Creach Bheinn** and **Fuar Bheinn** dominate this part of Morvern.

Fuar Bheinn and Creach Bheinn

The two Corbetts in Morvern, Fuar Bheinn and Creach Bheinn *(Map 6)* must have been close to these first activities of Somerled. Starting from Strontian, I drove up to the east end of Loch Sunart , whence I had contemplated going up Glen Tarbert and ascending Creach Bheinn by the Meall a'Bhainaiche ridge. However, I had some doubts about crossing the Carnoch River and decided to drive round to the south side of the Loch where I parked my car close to a small cottage. I called in to tell the occupant of my plans and had the good fortune to find that he had been a shepherd in the area for very many years. He advised me to climb Fuar Bheinn keeping to the east bank of the Allt na Creiche which was in full spate but which would have some fine waterfalls and I could cross it further up the hill if I wanted. There was a small track along the stream side and I soon reached the plateau area below Fuar Bheinn. I followed a ridge all the way to the summit where unfortunately I found myself deprived of the anticipated view over Ardgour and Sunart by a thick mist which swept over the tops. There was no trouble however, in descending to the Cul Mham bealach and a compass bearing enabled me to reach the top of Creach Bheinn. The mist suddenly cleared away leaving me with a superb view down Glen Galmadale. The whole of Loch Linnhe with Mull, Lismore and other islands was beautifully clear. On the way down, the mist to the north lifted, revealing the splendours of Sunart and Ardgour. The only blemish was the scar on the slopes of Ben Resipol resulting from the mining operations taking place above Strontian. On the way down torrential rain began to fall and I had to be very careful to ensure that I did not get on the wrong side of a stream which I would certainly not have been able to cross further down the hill.

Expulsion of the Norsemen from the Mainland

Somerled continued his successful attacks on the Norsemen until he had driven them from the mainland. Some of his skirmishes would probably have taken place in among the Ardgour Hills including Corbetts **Sgurr**

Somerled and the Norsemen

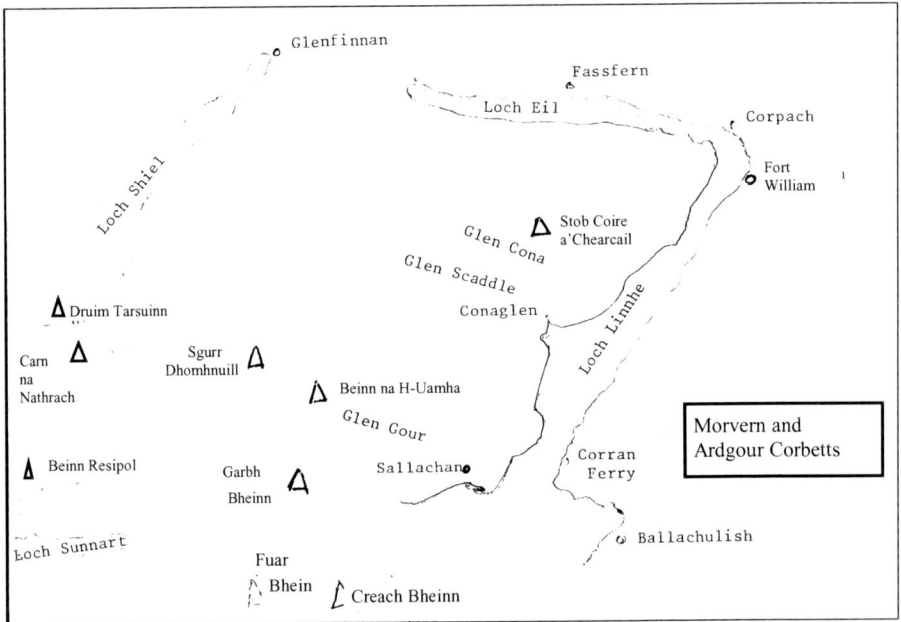

Map showing places including Glenfinnan, Fassfern, Loch Eil, Corpach, Fort William, Loch Shiel, Stob Coire a'Chearcail, Glen Cona, Glen Scaddle, Conaglen, Loch Linnhe, Druim Tarsuinn, Carn na Nathrach, Sgurr Dhomhnuill, Beinn na H-Uamha, Glen Gour, Corran Ferry, Beinn Resipol, Garbh Bheinn, Sallachan, Loch Sunnart, Ballachulish, Fuar Bheinn, Creach Bheinn. Box labelled "Morvern and Ardgour Corbetts".

Map 6

Dhomhnuill, Druim Tarsuinn and Carn na Nathrach (Druim Tarsuinn has now been renamed **Stob a Bhealach an Sgriodain**.).

One such skirmish took place near Acharacle, and Wendy Wood has described it in her book. Torcuil, the ancestor of the MacLeods of Lewis, and his Norsemen landed near Dorlin to ravage the Moidart coast and drove the local inhabitants back as far as Langal. But here, Somerled came to their rescue. Torcuil and his men were driven back to the ford over the River Sheil, where Torcuil was killed. The place was named after him; Ath Torcuil (the ford of Torcuil) now written as Acharacle.

Somerled and his men would probably have assembled in the Morvern and Ardgour areas near Corbett **Garbh Bheinn** and would have traversed the slopes of Corbett **Ben Resipol** en route to the fighting.

Druim Tarsuinn, Carn na Nathrach and Sgurr Dhomhnuill

I planned, if I could get permission, to go up the forest road in Glen Hurich to a bothy at Resourie as the ascents would be much more manageable from there. I contacted the Forestry Commission office at Strontian where I was given the key to the locked gate at the end of the

Somerled and the Norsemen

Ardgour – Carn na Nathrach from Druim Tarsuinn

forestry road and allowed to drive my car up to just above the bothy. I could see the bothy down below me in the forest but before going down I took the precaution to turn my car so that I was facing downhill - a wise move as it turned out.

Druim Tarsuinn (now renamed Stob a Bhealach an Sgriodain)

Having inspected the bothy there was still a few hours of daylight left. An attempt on Druim Tarsuinn was feasible. A rough track up to the Bealach an Sgriodain provided a good route to a ridge leading south east to the summit. In the failing light there was an excellent view of the two summits scheduled for the next day as well as the other summits of the Ardgour area. It was dark as we returned to the bothy but we quickly got a good fire going and enjoyed our evening meal in its warming flickerings.

Carn na Nathrach and Sgurr Dhomhnuill

A shock awaited us in the morning when we found an unexpected and considerable fall of snow had occurred during the night. Although we had come without ice-axes or crampons, we decided to attempt Carn na Nathrach and set off practically due south from the bothy switching to a north east bearing when we reached the ridge. By this time the snow was falling steadily and visibility was decreasing. We reached the summit cairn and after some discussion we decided to retrace our steps along the ridge and cut down the steep slope to the bealach at the head of Gleann na Cloiche Sgoilte where we would review the position. The descent was very steep and required great care in the snowy conditions. On reaching the bealach, we had no hesitation in abandoning any attempt on the steep ridge up to Druim Garbh in our unequipped state. We therefore reconciled ourselves to the long walk down Gleann na Cloiche Sgoilte to its junction with Gleann an Lochain Duibh. The snow storm increased in intensity as we battled our way along the glens to Lochain Dubh and up to Mam Beathaig. We were thankful to get into the upper end of Glen Hurich and even more thankful to get into the snugness of our bothy and its wood fire.

After a comfortable night in our bothy we woke to find no relaxation in the snowstorm and we decided to abandon any further climbing as we had come quite unprepared for snow conditions. Sgurr Dhomhnuill had to be left for another day.

I was keen to remedy my failure to climb Sgurr Dhomhnuill and I returned to Strontian for this purpose. Despite the low cloud base when I left Strontian, I thought the top could be attained. I drove up to the car park at Arriundle Nature Reserve and then cycled up to the beginning of the path to the disused lead mines where I left my cycle. I planned to proceed to Druim Leac a' Sgiathain, a ridge culminating in Sgurr na h'Ighinn. Continual compass work was required to keep on course. I duly reached the Ighinn summit and continued to Sgurr Dhomhnuill where I reached the summit area in about three hours from the lead mines. On the way down the outlines of Garbh Bheinn and Beinn Resipol could be picked out. The successful ascent had, alas, disappointing views but there was some compensation in the enjoyable cycle run through the Arriundle Nature Reserve with its great oak trees.

Garbh Bheinn

Sandy and I travelled to Strontian and hoped that the good weather conditions we were experiencing would continue for assaults on Garbh Bheinn and Ben Resipol. Our first choice was Garbh Bheinn for although it may not be the monarch of the Ardgour hills as regards height it is in my view the hill deserving of the title. We parked at the bridge over the Amhainn Coir'an Iubhair. We found a rough track starting about 100 yards west of the bridge and climbed steadily up Sron a Garbh Choire Bhig - with frequent stops for the heat. When we reached the Sron summit, the peak of Garbh Bheinn itself burst upon us with its fearsome looking cliffs. It looked as though we might have some interesting scrambling to reach the Garbh Bheinn summit. However when we got down to the bealach we found a straightforward route to the

Somerled and the Norsemen

Ardgour– Garbh Bheinn

summit. After contemplating a return route by Beinn Bheag, Sgor Mhic Eacharna and Druim an Iubhair, we lazily opted to return by the way we had come. In retrospect we regretted this decision as the views of the Garbh Bheinn cliffs from the other ridge would have been magnificent. It would have shown up the Great Ridge - a climb I would have liked very much to have taken on had I been less stiff. However we could not complain about Ardgour's treatment of us on its finest hill.

Ben Resipol

With the weather still set fair Ben Resipol was our next choice as it is such a wonderfully central viewpoint. After an early breakfast we drove to Resipol Farm and parked our car on the beach well above the tide level. We crossed the Allt Mhic Chiarain whence an excellent track took us comfortably up into the hill. Although it was quite warm, mist came down on the tops. However we followed the Allt Mhic Chiarain to a point where it divides. We took the right hand branch which led us to a very steep ascent to the summit. To our delight we had the rare pleasure of finding ourselves above the mist with the peaks protruding from a great woolly cloud base. Ben More, Beinn Tallaidh,

Somerled and the Norsemen

Dun da Gaoithe and all the Morvern and Ardgour tops could be identified. As we leisurely enjoyed this unusual type of view, the mist began to lift and revealed range after range of hills in all directions justifying the classification of Beinn Resipol as an outstanding viewpoint.

Somerled and Islay and Jura

Having evicted the Norsemen from the mainland, Somerled then turned his attention to the Isles. The Hebrides were then controlled from the Isle of Man by a Norse King, Olaf the Red, himself a vassal of the King of Norway, Magnus Barfod. Somerled requested Olaf the Red for the hand of his daughter, Ragnhilda, in marriage. But the proud King thought that his daughter deserved someone better than the young Gael. However Somerled was not to be denied and the marriage took place. Some years later Olaf was murdered in the Isle of Man by his nephews while his oldest son, Godred was in Norway. But Godred returned to the Isle of Man and in turn killed his cousins and became the new King of the Isle of Man. Soon, however, he and his brother-in -law, Somerled, disagreed and Somerled engaged and defeated him in a naval battle. This success was based on the excellent fleet which Somerled had built up incorporating a new and smaller type of galley. This smaller ship, called a 'nyvag' meaning little ship, was constructed with a hinged rudder and included a 'crows nest' on the mast for archers. These new galleys proved superior to the Norse galleys, 'skutas' as they were known. Somerled obtained control of the northern portion of the Hebrides leaving Godred in control of the southern portion down to the Isle of Man. Somerled based his fleet on Lagavulin Bay in Islay but in order to control the Sound of Islay he fortified the small islet, Am Fraoch Eilean, off the coast of Jura overlooking the Sound. In passing it is interesting to note that Donald, Somerled's grandson, built a castle overlooking Lagavulin Bay and called it Dunyveg – the castle of the little ships.

This situation did not last long and after a further disagreement, Somerled invaded the Isle of Man and again defeated Godred who fled to Norway. Somerled then became outright controller of the Western Scottish mainland, nominally as a vassal of the Scottish King, and of the whole of the Islands down to the Isle of Man, nominally as a vassal of the King of Norway.

Jura
Beinn an Oir

It was with Somerled's naval victory in mind that I turned my attention to the somewhat inaccessible Corbett in Jura, **Beinn an Oir** – one of the Paps. *(Map 7)* This involved a real expedition. A car drive to Tarbert in

Somerled and the Norsemen

Kintyre followed by a Caledonian MacBrayne ferry saw us in Port Ellen on a Sunday afternoon with no further transport available that day. The post bus on Monday morning deposited us in the attractive little township of Bowmore and a second post bus took us to Port Askaig. From here a 'tank landing' type of ferry crossed to Feolin where the Craighouse Hotel milk van took us to the very comfortable hotel. The manager kindly transported us to the Jura Forest Pier, which he recommended to us as a better starting point than the path up the side of the river from the Corran bridge. An ascent along the broad ridge brought us to Loch an-t-Siob where

Map 7

we followed the north shore. Unfortunately weather conditions had deteriorated and we decided not to complete the ascent of Beinn Shiantaich but contoured around its south west slopes until we reached the saddle below Beinn an Oir. A longer than expected ridge walk - with a superfluity of cairns - took us easily to the summit of Beinn an Oir. Sadly the thick misty conditions prevailed, and we decided to return by Loch an-t-Siob. We reached the road in about two and a half hours from the summit and had a somewhat weary walk down the road back to the hotel. We enjoyed some delicious venison for our evening meal. But if one can't get good venison on 'Deer Island' where can one get it.

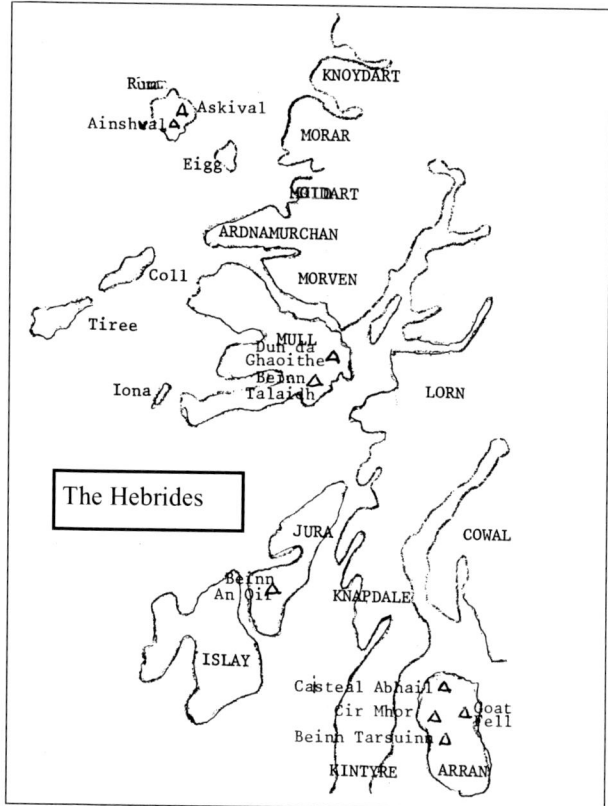

Somerled and the Norsemen

The Hills of Mull from Ulva

The Somerled Family and the Island of Mull

A rising took place against the Scottish King in support of the McHeth claimants to the throne who were possibly descendants of King Lulach and to whom Somerled was related by marriage. Somerled supported his relatives against the King but was assassinated during the campaign. Although after his assassination, his three sons, Ranald, Dougall and Angus split the Hebridean Island kingdom between them, Godred returned in force from Norway and regained control of the Isle of Man and the northern group of the Hebrides leaving the sons with the southern Isles and the Western Mainland. Sadly, the three sons quarrelled over the ownership of Mull and Arran. In a battle over this issue Angus and his own three sons were all killed and the remaining two Somerled sons Ranald and Dougall split his inheritance between them. It is worth noting that Angus's daughter married the eldest son of the Steward of Scotland and from this marriage sprang the Stewart Kings of Scotland and later Britain.

A later association of the Island of Mull with the Somerled family occurred during the Wars of Independence when Angus Og, great great grandson of Somerled, was joined in his support of Robert the Bruce by the Maclean family in Mull, who later became relations by marriage with the

Somerled group. Hector Maclean founded the Maclains of Loch Buie and Lachlan Maclean founded the Macleans of Duart.

It was in Mull, too that some of the final throes of the Somerled dynasty took place. Angus Og, son of John, Fourth Lord of the Isles, rebelled against his father. In a naval battle near Tobermory, Angus defeated his father and his supporters Maclean of Duart, MacLeod of Lewis and MacNeil of Barra.

The Corbetts of Mull
Beinn Talaidh and Dun Da Ghaoithe

With the Somerled family historical associations much in mind, a plan was prepared to climb **Beinn Talaidh** and **Dun da Ghaoithe** from a base in Oban, using the 8 a.m. ferry to Craignure. We ascertained from the Torosay estate keeper the evening before we went, that we would not be interfering with any estate activities on the two hills. The Iona bus from Craignure left at 9a.m. reaching Torness on the Lussa River about 9.15a.m.. From this starting point I had calculated that it should be possible to climb Beinn Talaidh, descend to Glen Forsa and climb up the south ridge of Coire nam Fuaran to the summit of Dun da Ghaoithe. From here I would proceed to the TV aerial and take the track down towards Torosay Castle reaching Craignure before the last ferry at 5p.m..

At Torness we found that the cloud level was fairly high, about 2250 feet and we had no difficulty in reaching the summit well within our schedule. However when the valley was reached my companion, unaccustomed to climbing, was too exhausted to face the steepish ascent up Coire nam Fuaran. A quick recalculation was made and we decided to start the long road walk to Craignure and estimated that we could make it in time for the last ferry, leaving Dun da Ghaoithe for another day.

Dun da Ghaoithe

My Munro enthusiast friend from England, Wilf, planned to climb Ben More and I had still to climb Dun da Gaoithe. So we planned a joint expedition based on Oban. We caught the first ferry to Craignure and found the Iona bus awaiting on the pier. Unfortunately it was not returning to Craignure that afternoon. Wilf decided to hitch a lift. I planned to walk from Cragnure to the top of Dun da Ghaoithe and back on my own. I set off on foot up the track to the TV aerial - the track I had planned to descend when I was with Tom on Beinn Talaidh. On the ascent, despite it being a Saturday, I met a group of road workers who told me that the TV track was being extended to get the aerial further up the hill so that it could have better contact with other aerials in the islands. At the TV aerial the mist had come down and the new track soon petered out. In the thick mist I was glad to find the OS Pillar and the huge cairn fairly quickly. So the summits of Mull denied me a view point for a third time as I had climbed Ben More also in thick mist. It was so thick and uninviting that I decided to return the same way but I have to confess to being rather casual in not taking careful bearings from the summit, contrary to my usual practice. I found myself on the steep south west slope of Mainnir nam Fiadh. I continued to traverse round the slope and eventually descended along the Beinn Bheag ridge. My casualness was punished as it was very heavy going over the moor to Lochan an Doire Dharaich whence I reached the Craignure road. Wilf, having ascended Ben More also in mist, and I foregathered at Craignure. He had had no difficulty in hitch-hiking.

The Knoydart Hills; Sgurr Coire Choinnichean and Beinn Bhuidhe

King Haakon's Expedition

The Battle of Largs

Early in the reign of Alexander II there was, as already mentioned, a rebellion on behalf of the McHeths, supported by the Somerled family. This did not endear the islanders to Alexander. He made several strong attempts to bring them under his control and in the midst of his last attempt he died on the island of Kerrera. The regents for his young son, Alexander III continued to exert pressure on the islanders to accept feudalisation and when Alexander III reached manhood he determinedly followed his father's policy. This created much unrest in the islands and a representative, one of the Somerled family, was sent to Norway to ask King Haakon to take action in support of the islanders who were regarded by the Norwegian King as his subjects. King Haakon agreed that matters were out of hand and assembled a large expedition of ships and men to sail to Scotland to remedy the situation.

In 1263, Haakon sailed with his large fleet for Scotland. It is stated in the saga which bears his name, that after rounding Cape Wrath, he anchored his fleet at Asleifarvik (called Oldshore Beg now) near Loch Inchard where the Norsemen must have gazed at the huge Corbetts, **Foinaven** and **Arkle**, from their anchorage. *(Map 8)*

Foinaven, Arkle and Meall Horn

As the seamen on Haakon's fleet must have done we gazed - in our case with admiration - on the magnificent range of hills, Foinaven and Arkle. The fascinating book, 'The Big Walks' by Wilson and Gilbert greatly tempted us to attempt the traverse of Foinaven and Arkle which is a walk of over 20 miles. A careful measurement of distances and heights however, made us realise that at our 'aged' walking speed it would be a bit beyond us. So we decided on the alternative of splitting the 'Big Walk' into Foinaven from the north and Arkle (and possibly Meall Horn) from the south.

Foinaven

We set off from near Gualin House to tackle Foinaven. A track somewhat badly broken up by tracked vehicles taking fishermen to their beat, leads off the road along Strath Dionard. We met the keeper to whom I had, some time earlier, written asking permission to traverse Foinaven and Arkle, which he had acknowledged, granting it. Naturally we asked his advice on the best route to adopt but, surprisingly, he had little knowledge of this side as the stalkers rarely came off the hill in this direction. He suggested that we should branch off the track before it went down to the river and contour round Cnoc a Mhadaidh onto the northwest slope of Ceann Garbh. This was the route which we had already decided ourselves to adopt so we graciously accepted his advice. It was a glorious day of sunshine and it was sweaty work going up the steep grassy slope leading to Ceann Garbh. The ground nearer the top was rather rocky and did not meet with much approval from my Labrador Francie. At the Ceann Garbh summit, the stupendous ridge of Foinaven and Arkle unfolded itself before us with a huge background of hills and lochs. It was easy to see why it had been included as one of the 'The Big Walks'. The ridge is quite narrow but presents no trouble in fine weather. Needless to say, the summit of Ganu Mor compelled a lengthy stop to take advantage of our luck with the weather.

Before coming, Hugh had, I told him, tempted providence by preparing a panorama of the view we could expect to get at Ganu Mor in clear conditions. His optimism and work were well rewarded. To the east Caithness's Morven, and possibly Scaraben also, could be picked out. Then Ben Wyvis, Ben Rinnes we thought, the Ben Dearg group, the Fannichs, around to the magnificent An Teallach. Closer by rose Ben Klibreck while shapely Ben Stack with its loch below made a picture postcard vista. Quinag, Suilven, Ben Hope, and a top of Ben Loyal, next door Beinn Spionnaidh and Cranstackie completed the circle of the superb Northern

King Haakon's Expedition

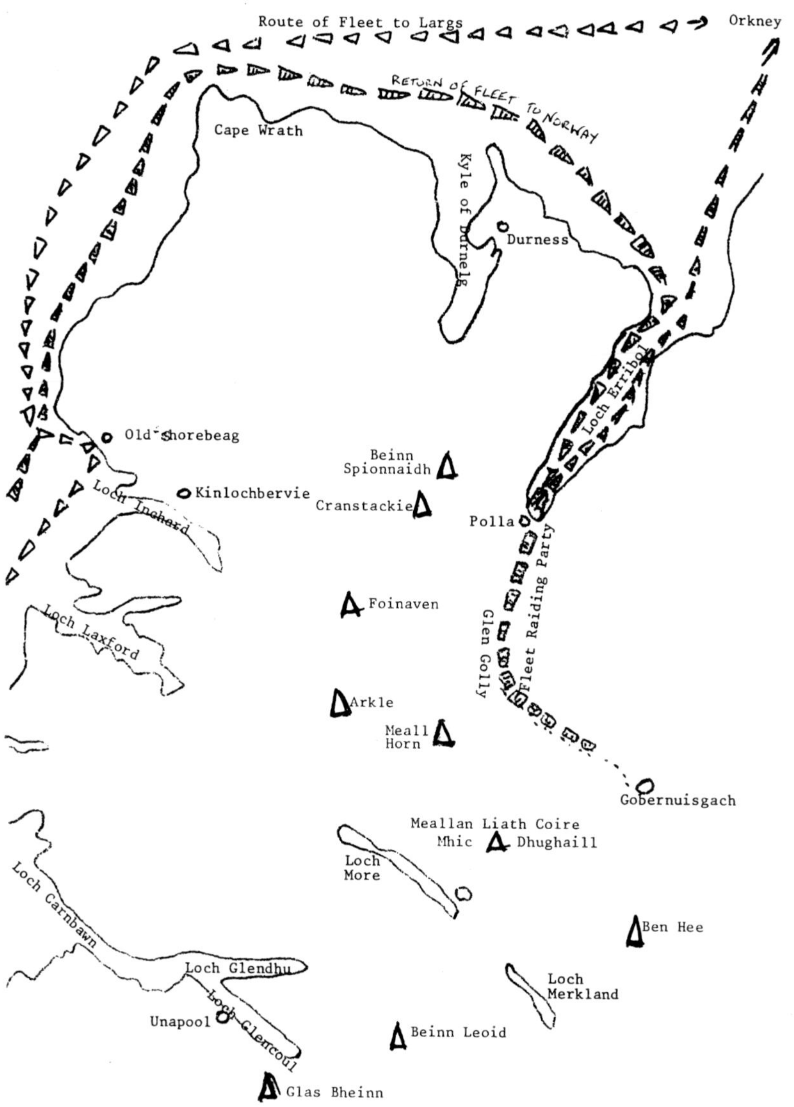

Hakon's Fleet en route to and from Largs

Map8

summits. Away to the north-west we picked up an island which we considered could only be the distant South Rona. Long stretches of Harris and Lewis were easily identified. The small villages of Rhiconich, Oldshore More, Oldshore Beg and Sheigra with Cape Wrath in the distance seemed quite close . Faraid Head and Whiten Head with Loch Eriboll glittering between them completed Hugh's panorama. It seemed almost too good to be true that we had been so lucky.

We then looked wistfully and longingly along the marvellous ridge leading to Arkle and Meall Horn and wished we had been here sixty years previously when we first started hillwalking together. Alas, after walking along to the subsidiary top above A Cheir Gorm, we had to turn back. As the weather was so fine we thought we would just go straight down to the road although the large number of small lochans suggested that we would have some rough and wet ground to cover. This proved to be the case and we agreed that our choice of the ascent route had been a much wiser one. As we passed Gualin House in the evening we left a message to our keeper friend that we had thoroughly appreciated his fine hill.

Arkle and Meall Horn

As we were in the stalking season, we had checked the night before from Mr.Anderson, the keeper at Ardachuilinn as to whether we might climb on Arkle and Meall Horn. We were delighted to learn that the next day's stalking was to be much further to the east and that we could certainly go climbing on Arkle. So far as Meall Horn was concerned we would have to check with him in the morning as it would depend on the wind direction. To this, of course, we readily agreed. We checked in early at Ardachuilinn the next morning and were delighted to hear that the wind direction was such that we could safely go on Meall Horn also. This is the kind of keeper-walker cooperation that would remove much of the problem of access and I have found it repeated on many other occasions.

We drove up a reasonable farm road from Ardachuilinn to the deserted steading called Lone. From here a good track leads up the side of the Allt Horn. About a mile up the track, we took to the ridge going up between two burns until we were looking down into An Garbh Coire. We continued round the sickle - shaped ridge, passing the lower of Arkle's tops, until we reached the main top. The splendid panorama we were beginning to expect unfolded before us. We returned along the ridge and aimed at the bealach below Creagan Meall Horn where we intended to go direct up the steep slope to the ridge. The slope was indeed steep and took longer and much more out of us than expected. Once up, a comfortably easy slope took us to the summit of Meall Horn. Views of the Inner and Outer Hebrides and of the Orkneys were particularly fine from here. But we were running behind the time schedule we had indicated to our hostess at Unapool House so we speedily descended to the car at Lone and got back in time to enjoy a superb meal of beautifully cooked fresh venison.

The Coigach Hills

As Haakon and his fleet sailed on from Asleifarvik, the remarkably shaped Suilven with its associates in Coigach, **Cul Mor, Cul Beag** and Ben Mor Coigach would provide another striking picture for the Norse sailors. *(Map 9)* W. H. Murray explains in his book 'The Companion Guide to the West Highlands', that Suil comes from the Norse word for a pillar and the name Suilven is thus a mixture of the Norse word and the Gaelic Bheinn.

Cul Mor

I had not read W. H. Murray's Guide when I came to tackle this hill. If I had I would have followed his advice and used the pass between Stac Polly and Cul Beag for the ascent. However Hugh and I decided to use the eastern approach from Knockan where we parked our car near the Tourist Information centre. From there an excellent stalker's path took us up to the plateau below the main summit. On the plateau we edged north-west to

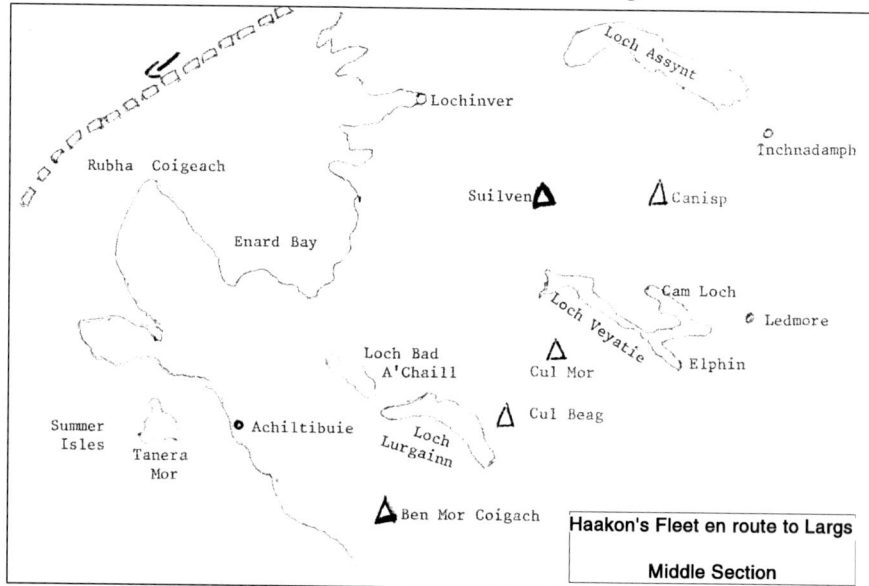

Map 9

enable us to climb the main summit Sron Garbh from the east. The final ascent was very steep and somewhat stony but presented no difficulty and I would agree with W. H. Murray's assessment that it is a rather dull approach. We had good viewing weather from the top and were able to see the slabby face of Breabag where we had had some difficulty. The views of the other Coigach hills and the Assynt hills were, needless to say, splendid and in the distance the Hebrides and to the east Ben Wyvis could be picked out. We descended the same way as we intended to climb Cul Beag later on in the day.

Cul Beag

We left Knockan and took the Achiltibuie road where we parked and set off up the south-east ridge of the hill. The weather conditions were still very fine and we had no difficulty in spotting the route up the ridge and quickly reached the summit by a steep final cone. The views from the top were naturally similar to those on Cul Mor but we got a good impression of the Cul Mor approach we could have taken from Loch Lurgain.

The Preparations and Strategy of Alexander III

The fleet continued south past the entrance to Loch Hourn and its Corbetts. Loch Hourn more than any other Loch must have reminded them of their native fiords but there is no record of their having sailed into it. They continued through the Kyle of Lochalsh, where Kyleakin is named after King Haakon. Eventually the fleet anchored at the Cumbraes offshore from Largs.

The Norwegian mobilisation had not gone unobserved in Scotland and Alexander III made preparations to repel the invaders by fortifying various strong points on the coast of Scotland. One of the points to which troops had been sent for this purpose is reputed to have been Inverie in **Knoydart** with the great Munros and Corbetts close to the village.

Alexander also mobilised a strong army of foot soldiers, archers and horsemen under the command of Alexander Stewart whose son, James, was a supporter of both Wallace and Bruce in the Wars of Independence. His grandson Walter, married Margery, daughter of King Robert the Bruce. This marriage produced the first of the Stewart Kings, Robert II.

The Knoydart Corbetts
Beinn Bhuide, Beinn na Caillich and Sgurr Coire Choinnichean

It had been with satisfaction that I had managed, in my seventies, to climb the 'big three' in Knoydart; Ladhar Bheinn, Luinne Bheinn and Meall Buidhe in a long day from Inverie and I wondered if some years later, I could somehow or other repeat the effort with the Corbetts. (*Map 10)* However

King Haakon's Expedition

when I examined the logistics it was beyond me. I thought I could climb Sgurr Coire Choinnichean in one outing with either Beinn Bhuidhe or with Beinn na Caillich but not with both. I therefore abandoned this objective, which incidentally illustrates the more distinct nature of the Corbetts compared to the Munros. Instead I decided to fit in my walks with the ferry schedule available between Mallaig and Inverie. I thought I could manage Beinn Bhuidhe on the day of arrival, take the whole of the next day to climb Beinn na Caillich and have time to climb Sgurr Coire Choinnichean before the ferry left the next day.

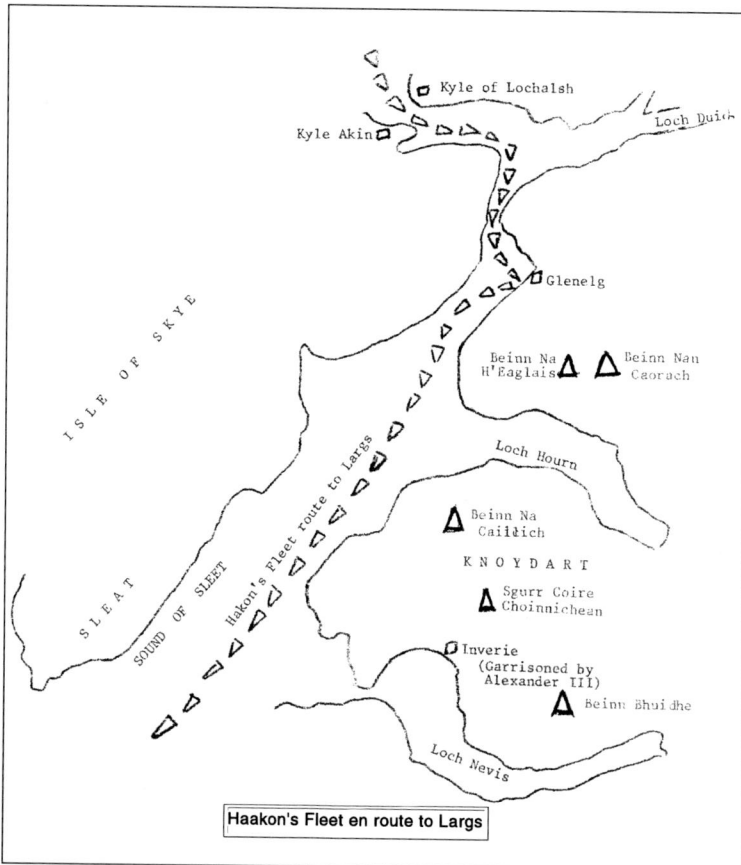

Map 10

King Haakon's Expedition

Beinn Bhuidhe

Having caught the early ferry to Inverie from Mallaig, I crossed the Inverie River into Gleann Meadaill and following a good path most of the way, I walked almost as far as Mam Meadail. I then struck up onto the Beinn Bhuidhe ridge and progressed along it to Mam Uchd. Rough ground over the top above Coire an t-Sagairt soon led to the summit of Beinn Bhuidhe. From here there were splendid views of all the Knoydart tops and also of the wild lochs Nevis and Morar. I continued along the fine ridge almost to Bealach Bhuidhe from where a very steep and rocky descent was made, back into Gleann Meadail to rejoin the outward track up the Gleann.

Beinn na Caillich

It was overcast and raining slightly during the ascent up the Allt a Mhuillin track down into Gleann na Guiserein. The weather showed signs of improvement and soon Beinn na Caillich was clear of mist although Ladhar Bheinn was still covered. The path up the east side of the Abhainn Bheag was followed but it was running very fast and was quite flooded. At the junction with Allt Coire Each the spate still prevented crossing and a long diversion up the stream was required before it could be forded. A traverse back to the Allt Mam Li was then needed. This stream was followed to the bealach to the east of the hill. In a sunny interval splendid views of Loch Hourn were obtained during the steady pull up to the mist covered summit. On account of the spate of the streams use of the bridge over the Abhainn Inbhir Guiserein seemed sensible and a south west bearing led over the outlier Meall Coire an t'Searraich down to the bridge and back onto the track back to Inverie. The total time for the walk was eight hours, rather more than we had planned.

Sgurr Coire Choinnichean

The ferry was due to leave at 14.45 p.m. but I felt this permitted sufficient time to climb the third Corbett. Starting directly from the village and in steady rain, a stalker's path led up the east side of the Allt Slochd Mhogha. The ridge on the east side of the Coire na Cloiche led through some interesting rocky ground to the summit. The rain had never stopped so there was no view to be obtained. An immediate descent in pretty damp clothing was quickly made to permit a change before the ferry boat arrived.

Battle of Largs

In 1263, Alexander stationed his army near Largs and entered into negotiations with Haakon. He cleverly protracted the negotiations until the weather began to deteriorate and Haakon's fleet was struck by a severe storm. The fleet was also getting short of supplies. The truce for negotiations ended and the Norwegians put ashore a strongly armed force but they were outnumbered by the Scots and could make no progress. Although the Norwegians were able to land reinforcements the effects of the storm and their lack of supplies prevented them from maintaining the pressure and the fleet had to withdraw. The Battle of Largs was probably not a major confrontation but it could be claimed to be a decisive victory as Haakon had to withdraw his fleet.

The Retreat of the Fleet to Norway

The Norwegian fleet retreated from the Cumbraes to Holy Island off Arran. They then decided to sail back to Orkney and thence back to Norway. After rounding Cape Wrath, they sent a raiding party ashore at Loch Eriboll, under the gaze of **Beinn Spionnaidh** and **Cranstackie**, to obtain provisions. (*Map 8*) Although the raiders penetrated as far inland as Glen Golly near the Corbetts, **Meall Liath Coire Mhic Dhughaill, Ben Hee and Beinn Leoid**, the local clansmen had withdrawn with their cattle and the Norsemen had to return to their galleys largely unsupplied and proceed to the Orkneys where King Haakon died. This proved to be a turning point in the history of the Hebrides since his successor on the Norwegian throne signed a treaty with King Alexander III at Perth formally ceding possession of the Hebridean Isles to Scotland. This ended Norwegian influence over the Hebrides . Alexander III had consolidated the Kingdom in its present day form apart from the Orkney and Shetland Islands whose eventual transfer took place some reigns later. Although the Norse control had been removed from the Hebrides the Lords of the Isles still maintained an almost separate regime from the Kingdom of Scotland and it was many years before they fully accepted the rule of the Scottish King. In Galloway too, a degree of independence continued but it was only a matter of time until the King exercised his authority over all these territories.

Cranstackie and Beinn Spionnaidh

We left Tongue for Durness in atrocious weather. However, the meteorological forecast was quite favourable. As we drove along the bleak shores of Loch Eriboll the prospect of good weather did not seem high. Nonetheless, we decided to make an attempt on Beinn Spionnaidh and Cranstackie starting at noon from Polla at the south end of Loch Eriboll. The ridge, north east of Beinn Spionnaidh, is called Carn an Righe - the hill of the king. A shepherd was busy with his sheep in the fold near where we parked our car and he told us that, despite the heavy rain, the streams were all fordable but a good distance up the hill. We set off north west up Beinn Spionnaidh and struck the main ridge north east of the top near Carn an Righe. Perhaps because of the mist and rain we found it to be one of these interminable ridges where there is always another top ahead. However we found the ordnance point, surrounded by a cairn, within the shelter of which we ate our sandwiches. The meteorologists were correct but it was only for a brief interval when there was a clearing of the mist and we caught a glimpse of Cranstackie and Loch Eriboll. The ascent from the col was very stony and much slower than we had anticipated . We descended, almost due east towards Polla, crossing the Abhainn an Uinnseinn fairly high up as the shepherd had recommended. The weather had never really cleared but we got some nice glimpses of Loch Eriboll as we descended.

The Loch More Group
Meallan Liath Coire Mhic Dhugaill

We made an early start from Unapool and reached Aultanrynie Lodge before 9 a.m.. A well made stalker's path provided easy access to about 1500 feet onto the broad whale back type ridge of Meallan Liath Beag. From there, as the name implies, a ridge which is rather stony, leads north west to the summit. In addition to the surrounding peaks, it was interesting to pick out Loch Shin, Loch Merkland, Loch a Ghriama, Loch Stack and a glimpse of Loch More as well as a number of smaller lochans. To the north -east lies Glen Golly with its unexpected historical associations with Haakon of Norway on his way back to Norway after the battle of Largs. The descent to Aultanrynle was uneventful and we enjoyed our snack sitting at the Lodge looking out over the glistening waters of Loch More.

Ben Hee

We thought there was still enough time left to climb Ben Hee and so we drove along to the north end of Loch Merkland. Here an old drove road runs up from the Loch along the east bank of the Allt nan Albannach and then through the Bealach nam Meirleach to Gobernuisgach Lodge at the head of Glen Golly. There are locked gates at the Loch Merkland end of the road but I had, a few days previously, called in at the Westminster Estate Offices at Achfary where we obtained permission to go on the hill and the factor kindly arranged for the gates to be unlocked for us. So we were able to drive ,with great care, up this old road to the bridge over the Allt Coire a' Chruiteir where we parked the car. A cairn, visible if you are looking for it, marks the start of a good path along the south side of the stream. This path led us almost directly to the southern and higher of Ben Hee's two tops. The weather then took charge. We were suddenly enveloped in a thick and freezing fog and could not even get a glimpse of Loch a' Ghorm- Coire nestling below the summit. It had not been a particularly hard day's walking but it was one of the few occasions when I succeeded in climbing two distinctly separate Corbetts on the same day - admittedly with the help of the car to take me from one to the other.

Ben Leoid

We were lucky with the weather as the cloud base was high. We doggedly ascended the good stalker's path going south from Allt Cean Lochan starting from a point south east of Kinloch, leading to the south slopes of Meall na Leitreach. From here we could see a series of cairns further ahead and we continued south west towards them and in due course picked up the path alongside Allt Strath nan Aisinnin coming up from Loch More. In due course we picked up the bealach we were aiming at above Loch Dubh. We took the steep slope up to the summit of Beinn Leoid where the clouds were high enough for us to see the route we had followed all the way. We also got good glimpses of Loch Glencoul, Loch Glendhu and Loch More.

St Mary's Loch looking towards St Mary's Chapel

The Wars of Independence

I picked three main areas with Corbetts or Donalds associated with the various Independence campaigns. The Ettrick and Moffat valleys are associated with William Wallace's guerilla activities and with the later campaign of Edward Balliol. Bruce had many associations with the Galloway hills in the earlier part of his own campaign. The third area, the Pass of Brander, is usually associated with Bruce who defeated there the McDougalls, supporters of Comyn, his rival for the throne. It is less commonly associated with William Wallace who fought and won a battle there against the English .

The Wars of Independence arose with the deaths of Alexander III and his sole direct heiress, his granddaughter, the Maid of Norway. There were a number of claimants to the throne, mostly derived from David of Huntingdon, a younger brother of Malcolm IV and William the Lion. Edward I of England had long harboured ambitions to take over Scotland and took advantage of the dissension among the Scots as to the succession. He agreed to act as arbitrator and cleverly stipulated with each claimant that, should he be selected, he would pay homage to Edward as overlord of Scotland.

After considerable discussion Edward ruled that John Balliol was properly entitled to be the next king. Balliol was duly crowned, not by the hereditarily entitled Macduff, but by Edward's own representative. After enduring a humiliating overlordship for some time Balliol formally renounced his act of homage, an act which had never been homologated by the Scottish nation.

The incensed Edward then invaded Scotland with a strong army and dethroned Balliol, who was eventually exiled to his French properties. Edward went as far north as the Moray Firth receiving en route a large number of written promises of fealty to him - the Ragman's Roll - from the Scottish nobles and other dignitaries. The roll did not include Wallace and his fellow leader Moray.

On Edward's arrival in London the flags were flying to celebrate the conquest of Scotland. The conquest was however a nominal one as although he received promises of fealty from some thousands of nobles and clerics, the common people had never agreed to the capitulation. Among the dissenting section of the nation was William Wallace.

Sir William Wallace, Guardian of Scotland

William Wallace was the second son of a minor knight, Sir Malcolm Wallace of Elderslie who was in the service of the Steward of Scotland. Wallace soon registered his antipathy to the English domination by acts of violence against members of the English garrisons at places like Dundee and Lanark. He steadfastly supported John Balliol whom he considered to be the rightful king of Scotland and all his actions were taken in support of King John, unworthy though he was. He was well supported by the common people but the nobles were always, apart from some notable exceptions like Alexander Moray, Neil Campbell, Alexander Scrimgeour, and William Douglas, reluctant to be led by the son of a minor knight. In any event many of them had large properties in England which they were probably unwilling to jeopardise.

After his early brawlings with the English garrisons in the Ayrshire area, Wallace took refuge in Ettrick Forest and no doubt traversed the many hills comprising **the Ettrick Donalds**. *(Map 11)* At this stage he appears to have been chosen by the commune of Scotland to lead the fight against the English and it has been suggested that he was nominated as Guardian of Scotland at St. Mary's Chapel near St. Mary's Loch.

The Donalds of Ettrick Forest

The Donalds in this area can be conveniently divided into two sections, namely those to the north of the Bodesbeck Burn and those to the south. It was probably the north group that Wallace and his men were most likely to frequent and I decided to make a day outing from Edinburgh to walk over that group. They include Bodesbeck Law, Bell Craig, Andrewhinney Hill, Mid Rig, Trowgrain Middle, and Herman Law. This attractive ridge, really almost a terrace, lies between the Moffat water to the west and the Ettrick Water to the east with the Moffat Water running south towards Moffat and the Ettrick running north towards Selkirk.

My plan was to leave my folding cycle at the head of the Moffat Water valley, close to the cottage with the plaque commemorating the famous geologist, Charles Lapworth, who carried out considerable research into the geological structure of the valley. It was a lovely day when I drove along the shore of St. Mary's Loch passing the site of the old chapel and recalling the suggestion that it was here that Wallace was proclaimed Guardian of Scotland. I duly parked my cycle behind the cottage and drove down to Bodesbeck Farm where I parked my car. I walked up the track to the col between Bodesbeck and Potburn. Here I took to the hills and soon reached the top of Bodesbeck Law. There were no navigational problems, as not only was it fine weather, but a fence led along the ridge to point 1991 and on to Bell Craig and Andrewhinney Hill. The ridge makes a splendid viewpoint all the way along and I preferred the views to the west where Carrifran Gans, White Coomb and of course the Grey Mare's Tail and Loch Skeen made a fine prospect. In the far distance I could pick out the line of the Cheviots. The Moorfoots also could be identified. The Ettrick valley was below me to the east with Peniestone Knowe above Ettrick village, looking much more than its 1807 feet, and the old Border favourites, the Eildons and Ruberslaw were all

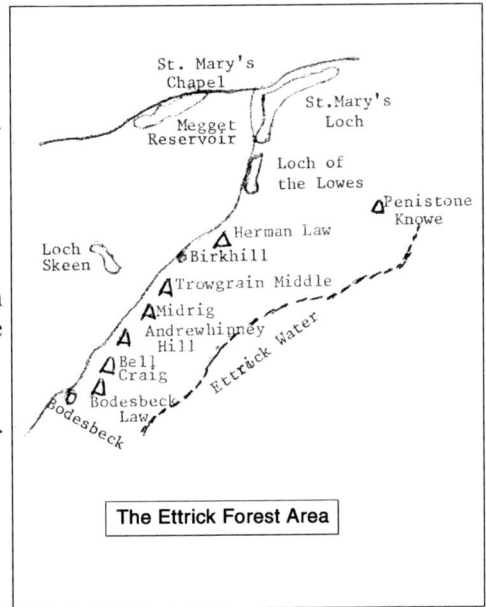

The Ettrick Forest Area

Map 11

clearly seen. I continued along the ridge past Mid Rig, Trowgrain Middle and Herman Law. From here it was a convenient descent to my folding cycle and the whole walk made a very enjoyable outing of four hours. This was clearly the best direction for me to have taken as the cycle run down the valley was really splendid.

Wallace's Campaign

During this period, Wallace actively engaged the English forces. Like Bruce after him, he defeated an English force at Loudon Hill. He then captured Scone, invested the castle at Dundee along with Alexander Scrimgeour and captured Stirling Castle. Wallace later, in his capacity as Guardian, nominated Scrimgeour to be hereditary standard bearer of Scotland. While he was at Stirling he received a plea for help from his strong supporter, Sir Neil Campbell of Lochow, ancestor of the Dukes of Argyll and conducted a successful battle against the English forces at the Pass of Brander. Shortly after, there occurred his famous and completely unexpected victory at Stirling Bridge. This infuriated Edward so much that he returned from his continental campaign and led an army himself to defeat the Scots and also with the purpose of capturing Wallace. He succeeded in defeating but not capturing Wallace at Falkirk largely due to the lack of support from the Scottish cavalry under Comyn.

Wallace was later betrayed to the English king by Sir John Menteith. The suggestion that the Lake of Menteith is named as the only Lake in Scotland because of this traitorous act is a romantic but unfounded idea. Wallace was given a so-called trial in England but it was a travesty and he was barbarously executed by Edward I. However the torch of freedom he had lit for Scotland was never extinguished thereafter.

The Crowning of Robert the Bruce

After the death of Wallace, Edward I installed his nephew, John of Brittany as a type of Vice-Roy of Scotland and kept the Scottish castles under English control. But Robert Bruce had other ideas and formed a secret pact with Lamerton, the Bishop of St.Andrews to aim at the independence of the Scottish nation with himself as king and the independence of the Scottish church. Thereafter, Bruce had himself crowned at Scone by a Countess of the MacDuff family. News of this crowning enraged Edward I who decided for a third time to invade Scotland to reduce that kingdom to English vassaldom. The first battle at Methven Woods was a resounding English victory and Bruce fled westwards to reach Kintyre to shelter with Angus Og - head of the branch of Somerled's dynasty who supported him.

After a period of recuperation in Kintyre, Bruce returned to his native Carrick and from there took refuge in the wild country around Glen Trool. Here he defeated the English troops at Loch Trool where he controlled the heights of **Lamachan**. This relatively small but successful engagement was followed by an encouraging victory in open country at Loudon Hill where Wallace had had a successful affray some years previously.

Bruce next turned his attention to the McDougalls of Lorn who were supporters of his rival claimants to the throne, the Comyns. At the Pass of Brander under Cruachan's mighty slopes, and quite near Wallace's battle some years before, he decisively defeated them. This encounter ended any threat to Bruce's throne from the McDougall support of the Comyns.

The Loch Trool Hills

During his sojourn in the Glen Trool area, Bruce had several successful skirmishes against the English and he and his men must have got to know well the hills on either side of the Loch; the great **Merrick range** to the north, commonly known as **the Awful Hand**, and the attractive group of hills, **the Minigaff Hills**, to the south of the Loch. (*Map 12*)

The Minigaff Hills
Larg Hill, Lamachan and Curleywee

It was on the lower slopes of Lamachan that Bruce's men ambushed and defeated a strong force of English troops sent out with the objective of capturing Bruce himself. Bruce is said to have controlled the battle from the north side of Loch Trool and there is a memorial stone there to record the occasion.

After studying the route from the maps, I decided that I could drive down to the Caldons camp site near Bargrennan from Edinburgh and drive back to Edinburgh in the evening.

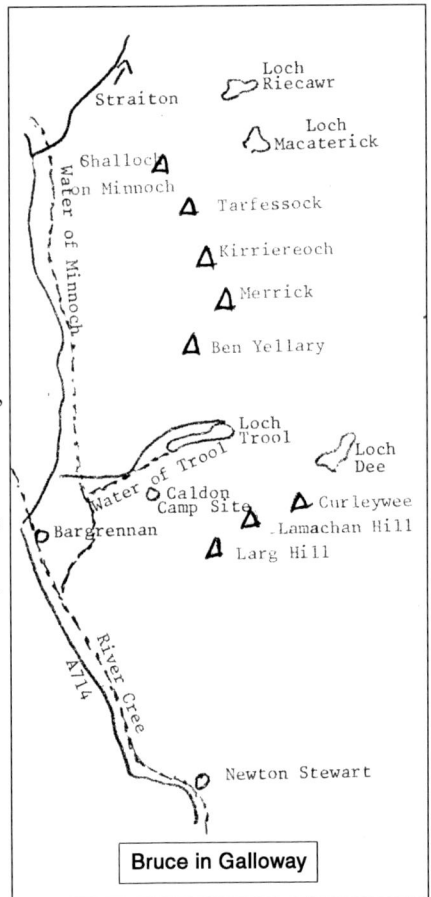

Map 12

58

The Wars of Independence

I reached the Caldon's site and went in to ask the camp warden if I might leave my car in his grounds. He and his wife proved most knowledgeable and helpful and, when he saw that I was using a 1933 map, insisted on my taking the modern version with me. I followed the good path which the warden had indicated to me along the right-hand side of the Caldon Burn until it forked when I took the right hand fork and soon reached the col between Lamachan and Larg Hill.

It had been a lovely walk up through the wooded area with a few delightful little waterfalls on the way up and I was looking forward to some nice panoramas from the three summits. Sadly as I reached the summit of Larg Hill a light mist came down and I had to content myself with the cairn alone. A compass reading was needed to take me to the top of Lamachan which I reached in two and a half hours from the camp site. Here I was lucky and there was a clear interval during which I could pick out the route to Curleywee without needing my compass. There is a splendid little ridge walk along to the Curleywee summit which was reached in three and a half hours including a sandwich stop. The visibility was a little better by now and as I descended the White Hill ridge towards Loch Dee I got some attractive views of the Loch itself and the three other ranges on my list, the Awful Hand with Merrick and its associates, Craignaw and Mullwharcher and the length of the Rhinns of Kells. It was a pleasant descent down to the road leading to Black Laggan bothy but I turned north-west along the shores of the Loch down the Glenhead Burn to Glenhead. Here I had intended to take the rough track along the south side of the Loch back to the Caldons camp site as this would have been through the site of the battle in 1306. But by now the mist had fallen and had brought persistent rain with it and so I rather reluctantly decided to return to the camp site by the main road. I reached the camp site in about six and a half hours and thanked the warden, duly returning his modern map.

The Merrick Range – The Awful Hand
Shalloch on Minnoch, Tarfessock, Kirriereoch Hill, Merrick and Ben Yellary

Sandy and Murray agreed to tackle the ridge with me enabling two cars to be used. We left one car at Bruce's stone in Glen Trool and drove in the other car to the highest point of the Bargrennan-Straiton road where we parked the second car, at point marked 1421 on my map.

We struck up over some tufted ground to Shalloch on Minnoch north top. The weather had been quite good when we set out but for a short time the mist came down and we had to make careful compass readings on this somewhat featureless part of the ridge. It was clear when we reached

Shalloch on Minnoch main top and we could see the route to Tarfessock and Tarfessock south top. Continuing along the tops we reached the top of Kirriereoch in three hours from the road. We descended to the col between Kirriereoch and Merrick to have some lunch but to our surprise we were struck by an influx of midges. Our lunch sandwiches were very quickly devoured and we set off up the Fang of Merrick. I had read that the Fang was possible to experienced hill walkers but my two companions had had some hesitations when we looked at the map before starting out. However, in good conditions, the Fang did not present us with any problems. Once up the Fang the summit was quickly attained; in three and a half hours from the start. In addition to the local hill ridges we could clearly identify Ailsa Craig and the Grey Hill near Girvan. The Arran Hills were just discernible in the haze but the views of the Lochs nearby were entrancing. We enjoyed the leisurely walk over to Ben Yellary savouring all the delightful scenery around us and were very much looking forward to our coffee we had left in the car at Bruce's stone.

Beinn a Bhuiridh

The Corbett, Beinn a Bhuiridh is associated with the battles fought in the Pass of Brander by both Wallace and Bruce *(Map 13)*. In earlier days I had traversed the magnificent Ben Cruachan ridge but my 'bible' of these days, the 1933 revision of the original 1921 Scottish Mountaineering Club General Guide, did not include the Corbetts and the Donalds and so I had never contemplated including Beinn a Bhuiridh in my round. Nor, of course had the great Cruachan reservoir been built. It was therefore with much interest that I returned to climb the Corbett. We took advantage of the offer of a lift up to the reservoir car park from which point we proceeded directly up to the summit of the Corbett impeded only by a few flurries of snow. The higher levels of Ben Cruachan were by then thickly covered with snow and made a wonderful background to the reservoir.

Beinn Chuirn, Beinn Udlaidh and Beinn Bhreac-Liath

When I was planning to climb these Corbetts, associated with Wallace's dash over to help his friends in Lorn and with Bruce's skirmish with the Mcdougalls at Dalrigh, I was struck by the nearparallelism of the three Glens – Strae, Orchy and Lochy up to the main Tyndrum to Blackmount road. Glen Lochy I noted was bordered by three Corbetts; **Beinn Chuirn** on the south side and **Beinn Udlaidh** and **Beinn Bhreac-Liath** on the north side. It is rarely possible to complete a group of three

The Wars of Independence

Beinn Laoigh and Beinn Chuirn

Corbetts in one day and I thought that I might make an attempt to climb these three in one go. However I did not plan it well. From the map I was doubtful about crossing the River Lochy and decided that I would leave my car on the roadside where the railway bridge crosses the river so that I would have no difficulty in getting over. My friend who was intent on achieving the 'four Munro' walk over Beinn Laoigh came with me to leave my car as planned and then kindly gave me a lift to South Tyndrum station. From here we enjoyed a pleasant walk up to Coninish. From there I took a route up past Eas Anie which proved to be rather steep. The weather was excellent and I spent a good half-hour on the summit of Beinn Chuirn admiring Beinn Laoigh with its snow filled gullies, Ben More and its satellites, the Beinn Dorain group and magnificent Ben Nevis fully snow clad. Had I been sure of crossing the River Lochy a direct but steep descent would have been possible in line with the summit of Beinn Udlaidh. But because of the uncertainty I took the route towards the railway bridge where I had left my car. After a short rest and some refreshment I faced the short but steep ascent to the Beinn Udlaidh whaleback ridge where a long walk took me to the summit with its large cairn. I was then faced with a time problem. It would not have been possible for me to climb Beinn Bhreac-Liath and return to my car in time to meet my four-Munro friend at the Beinn a'Cleibh road-end on completion of his climb as I had promised. Had I thought it out more carefully I could have left my car much nearer Beinn Bhreac-Liath and it would then have been possible to fulfil my promised meeting time. I was not particularly worried about Beinn Bhreac-Liath which can be easily ascended en passant, from the Tyndrum road. I was disappointed, however that one of the rare chances of climbing a group had been spoilt.

Some time later, I stopped at the Coire Chalein bridge on the Tyndrum road just south of the Auch railway horseshoe and following up the stream skirting the forestry plantation, quickly reached the omitted summit. The snow covered peaks around were a splendid reward for the extra effort and the snow also helped with some nice glissades on the way down.

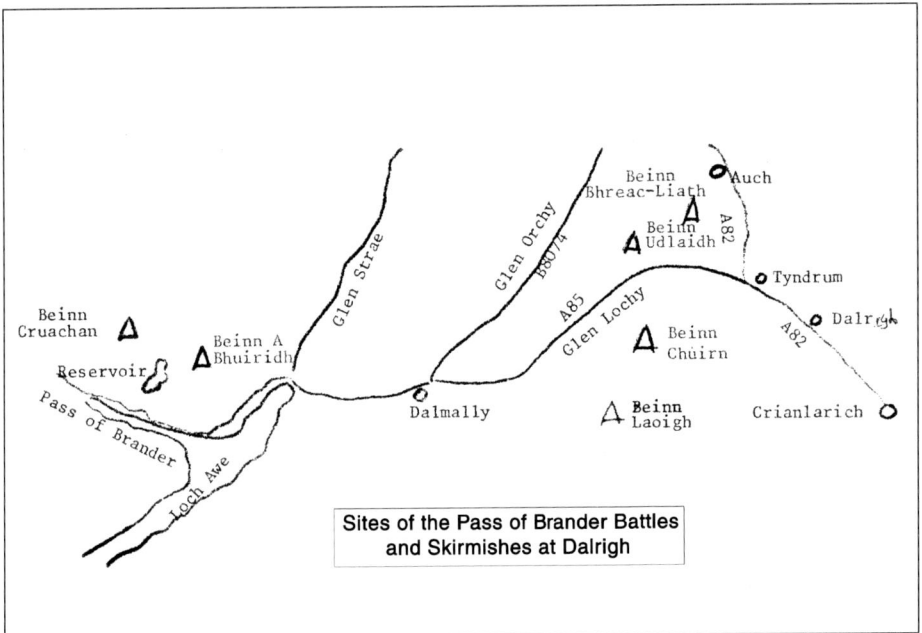

Map 13

The Wars of Independence

Edward Balliol's Attempt on the Throne

After the decisive battle of Bannockburn, desultory fighting across the Border took place on both sides until in 1328 the Treaty of Northampton was signed by the two countries. Although this recognised the independence of Scotland, it did not keep the English King from continuing to wish to dominate Scotland, and he supported an attempt to place Edward Balliol, son of King John Balliol, on the Scottish throne. The Balliol army landed in Fife and surprisingly defeated a superior Scottish force under the Regent, the Earl of Mar, at Dupplin Moor. In a very short time, Balliol had consolidated his position to the extent that he was crowned King at Scone by the Earl of Fife, the heriditary enthroner. After his enthronement Balliol paid homage for the Kingdom of Scotland to Edward III at Roxburgh. But almost immediately after this act of homage Balliol was ambushed at his camp at Moffat near **the Ettrick Donalds** and was forced to flee in complete disarray to the safety of Carlisle. For the time being the campaign halted. The Scottish force who surprised him at Moffat possibly used the Ettrick valley for their approach and I have associated the southern portion of the Ettrick Donald's with this episode.

Southern Ettrick Donalds

It was a day with bright intervals when I left Edinburgh and drove up the attractive Ettrick valley to the end of the tarmacadamed road and parked the car at Potburn. I then took the easy track up to the bealach between Bodesbeck Law and White Shank where I turned south along the ridge to White Shank. A further three and a half hour's pleasant walking along the tops took me via Smidhope Hill to Capel Fell. Here I made a very steep descent down some scree to the valley of the Selcoth Burn followed by a correspondingly steep ascent to the top of Croft Head. From here I again descended to the valley and had my lunch in a sheepfold not far from the Southern Upland Way which passes along here. Then an ascent once again to West Knowe, the Loch Fell west top and on to the main top. The ridge then was followed along by Wind Fell and Hopetoun Craig to Ettrick Penn with its massive cairn. I spent a short time here hoping for a clearer view but the visibility remained rather hazy and I descended to the valley again and walked back to the car. It was quite remarkable that I could walk all day on these hills which are not so far from Edinburgh and never meet a single person all day although at times, far below me I could see one or two walkers making their way along the Southern Upland Way.

The Wars of Independence

The End of the Wars

The campaign resumed the following year when Edward III sent a strong force which captured Berwick and inflicted a second and severe defeat on the Scottish army at Halidon Hill. This defeat, following that at Dupplin Moor, almost cancelled all the efforts Robert I had made to secure independence. But despite these major military defeats, strong pockets of resistance remained, among them being Kildrummy Castle, which was held by none other than Christian, sister of Robert Bruce, wife of Alexander Moray.Moray, the son of Wallace's fighting colleague who had died of wounds received at the battle of Stirling Bridge, was Regent for the young King David I, who had been sent to France for safety. Christian Bruce refused to surrender to the besieging Balliol army and sent a message to her husband for help. Her husband defeated the Balliol army and killed its leader at Culblean Hill near Ballater. Moray continued a successful campaign against the English army for two more years. This effectively brought the attempt on the throne by Edward Balliol to an end, enabling Scotland to hold grimly on to the independence for which it had so fiercely fought.

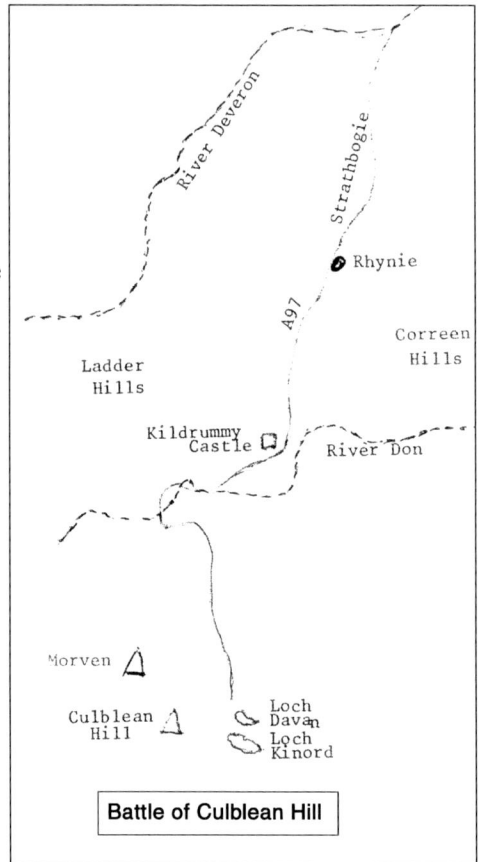

Battle of Culblean Hill

Map 14

Morven

This Corbett is linked with the important Battle of Culblean Hill (*Map 14*) where the Scottish victory over Edward Balliol did so much to ensure the independence of the nation. It is a hill which can be tackled almost as one passes by. In early May, Hugh and I, en route from Edinburgh to Boat of Garten, decided to divert a little from the Braemar -Tomintoul road and climb Morven. It was raining heavily when we reached the outskirts of Ballater where we branched north along the east bank of the River Gairn. At a farm called

The Wars of Independence

Lary, we followed the west bank of the Lary Burn until we were almost at the ruined outbuildings of the unoccupied Morven Lodge. Shortly before the lodge we found a good path which after we had managed to cross the burn, led along the south flank of Morven. Some way along this path we found a stalker's track by a line of butts leading up onto the main ridge. This we followed and soon reached the summit where an old boundary fence crosses the top of the hill. Partly because of the weather - we had a series of heavy snow showers passing over - and partly owing to the lie of the land there was not a striking view from the summit. We could look over to the south east towards Loch Davan where the decisive battle was fought but it all looked so peaceful and pleasant that it was difficult to imagine.

The site of the Battle of Culblean is not marked on my old map and this leads me to think that it's importance has only recently been appreciated. Sir Andrew Moray deserves a better historical press than he has so far received. The battle has however, been well researched and the alternative hypotheses by Dr. Simpson, Mr Wyness and by Professor Nicholson have been interestingly described by Marren in his book 'Grampian Battlefields'.

The Lowther Hills

James IV and his Foot Pilgrimage

James IV was 15 in 1488 when he succeeded to the throne. After a short Regency he took over the Kingdom and was able at long last to end the continual strife between King and nobles. The number of nobles who perished with him at the battle of Flodden is striking, if tragic, testimony to his success in this area.

During James IV's reign in Scotland, Henry VII of England wished for peace between the countries, and in due course this objective was encouraged by the momentous marriage of James IV to Margaret Tudor, Henry's daughter. Momentous in that it was from this marriage that James VI, their great-grandson, became King of both Scotland and England. Sadly the peace loving Henry VII was succeeded by Margaret's hot-headed brother Henry VIII and the brothers-in-law soon quarrelled. James renewed the Scottish alliance with France, invaded England in support of his ally, and lost his life at the disaster of Flodden.

The Foot Pilgrimage of James IV to Whithorn

The Foot Pilgrimage made by James IV to St. Ninian's Shrine at Whithorn

In 1507, James IV was worried about the health of his wife, Margaret Tudor and their newly born heir and decided to make a pilgrimage on foot to St. Ninian's shrine at Whithorn. (*Map 15*) He travelled from Edinburgh by Dolphinton and Lamington to Crawford. He then continued to Leadhills and from there crossed the hills to Durisdeer. After Durisdeer he crossed the Nith and went on to Dalry, Penningham, Wigtown and finally Whithorn. He felt that his effort had been worthwhile as Margaret recovered and indeed later accompanied him herself on a return visit to Whithorn. James also made several other pilgrimages, a number of them to the Tain area, but his foot pilgrimage to Whithorn is an outstanding feat for a reigning monarch.

In this remarkable pilgrimage on foot, James IV passed and actually traversed several Donalds. As mentioned above he walked by Dolphinton and Lamington and passed the lower slopes of **Tinto Hill** and the nearby **Culter Fell** group. Going on to Crawford he walked to Leadhills and crossed over **the Lowther Hills** to Durisdeer. Proceeding from Durisdeer to Penpont and Dalry he would be close to the northern section of the **Queensberry group**.

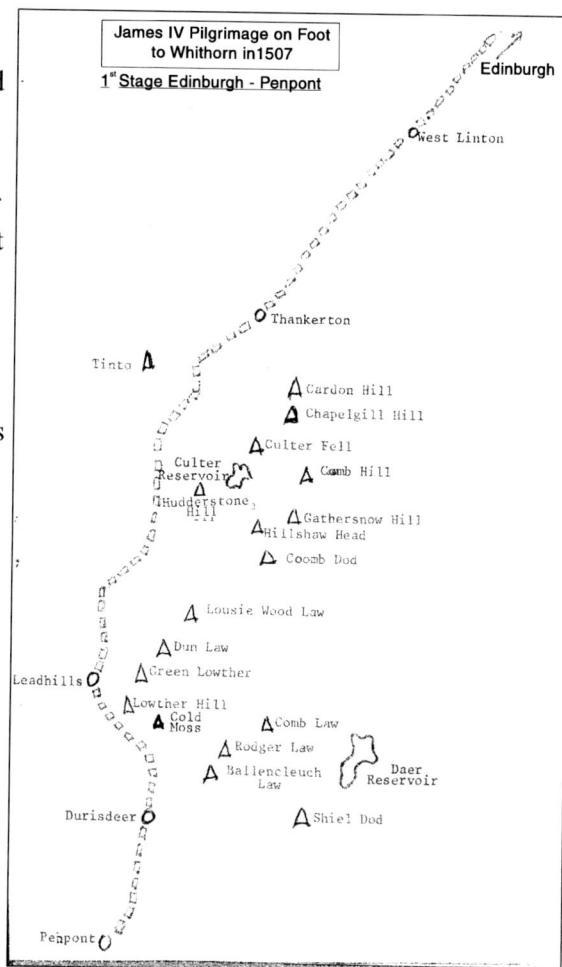

Map 15

He continued from Dalry to Penningham and Wigtown and finally to the shrine at Whithorn.

Tinto

James IV in the course of his pilgrimage must have been close to Tinto and it is interesting to speculate if his route was similar to that taken by the Jacobites, nearly 250 years later, in their retreat from Derby. Their route took them by the Douglas Water towards Glasgow and may have been further to the west. The very isolation of Tinto reinforces its position as an landmark visible from all around and it demands an ascent. The route which I took, many years ago, was to park my car on the Douglas Water-Wiston road and walk up to Howgate Mouth where I turned east over Lochlyock Hill and in a relatively short time reached the summit of Tinto. This is another of these so many pleasing little half-day excursions which can be undertaken from the Scottish capital and provides, on a good day, an excellent viewpoint for the surrounding area.

The Culter Fell Group

This group consists of five Donalds, Culter Fell, Chapelgill Hill, Gathersnow Hill, HillshawHead and Heatherstane Law and three associated tops Coomb Hill, Coomb Dod and Cardon Hill.

Hudderstone Hill (or Heatherstane Law)

It gave me pleasure to be able to ascend this Donald accompanied by my grandson, John, then aged about sixteen. We took the car up to the Culter reservoir and walked up onto Snowgill Hill and then on to the top of the Donald. It had been quite pleasant brisk walking weather when we set out and we had intended to continue along the ridge to Hillshaw Head at least. But as we reached the top it started to snow heavily and it soon turned to rain and thick mist so we made a straightforward retreat down The Bank to the south east end of the reservoir and walked round to the car .

Culter Fell, Gathersnow Hill, Coomb Hill, Hillshaw Head and Coomb Dod

I thought that the round of this pleasant group would be an opportunity to make a check on my walking speed in average walking conditions. There was a considerable amount of snow on the ground and the wind was extremely cold and strong but the weather was quite bright and even sunny at times.

The car was left just beyond Birthwood, where King's Beck stream flows into Culter Water. A steady climb of one and three quarter miles and 1600 feet up the ridge on the south side of King's Beck led to the summit of Culter Fell. The Lanarkshire – Peeblesshire boundary fence was then followed all the way to Glenwhappen Rig where a short subsidiary ridge led off to Coomb Hill – a further two and a half miles and 750 feet of climbing. From Coomb Hill I retraced my steps to Gathersnow Hill and over it to Hillshaw Head. The ridge was followed on to Coomb Dod into the strong wind all the way along the ridge of two and a quarter miles plus 500 feet of climbing. A return was then made along the ridge intending to cut down by the east side of Back Burn but ended up on the steep sided valley of the Back Burn which had to be traversed with some difficulty in the snowy conditions. The car was reached in two and a quarter hours from Coomb Dod - 5 miles and about 150 feet of climbing. According to the formula that I had designed for my mid-seventies I should have taken six and a half hours. The actual time I took was six and a quarter hours.

Chapelgill Hill and Cardon Hill

One Sunday in March, I elected to proceed to the two Culter Fell Hills which I had not yet climbed. After reaching Biggar and before reaching Culter I cut off by Hartree farm and Knoweshead farm and joined the Peeblesshire – Lanarkshire boundary fence near East Mains. I went up over Shaw Hill and down into the Culter Water valley passing the ruined Threepland Backshaw house en route. Further to the right was the ruined Cow Castle. The boundary fence was followed up over Black Hill and Scawdsmans Hill to the ridge of Cardon Hill. It was in thick mist at this height. In a heavy snow fall and in the teeth of a strong wind I left the boundary fence and took a compass bearing direct to the top of Chapelgill Hill. It was too cold and misty to linger on the top so I returned on the same bearing to the Cardon Hill ridge where I had little difficulty in reaching the Cardon Hill top in about half an hour. I descended towards Kilbucho Castle ruins and found myself back in the sunshine. Continuing round by White Hill the boundary fence was rejoined and a steep pull up Shaw Hill saw me back at the car. This round would be a very attractive one in good visibility.

Lowther Hills

This group of hills can be grouped into those north-west of the Dalveen Pass and those to the south east of the Pass. (*Map 15*) Bill and I decided to walk along the north-west Lowther ridge one sunny September day. Probably the easiest approach is to go up from the village of Wanlockhead but the plan we adopted was to take a folding cycle in the boot of the car and drive up to the top of the Dalveen Pass and leave the folding cycle there. We then drove down again and parked the car at Glenlochar Farm. This enabled us to walk comfortably along the ridge and then I freewheeled down on the cycle to bring the car up to the top of the pass. This plan worked very well indeed.

From the farm we ascended onto the ridge over Coupland Gair to the rounded top of Lousie Wood Law and then over the small rise of White Law to Dun Law and Dungrain Law. Another small rise, Peden Law, was then crossed to lead to Green Lowther, the highest of the whole Lowther group. Probably because of its height the Postal authorities have established a radio and telephone reinforcer on the hill while its neighbouring top, Lowther itself, is 'blessed' with a radar station which requires the presence of large white domes visible from miles away. Strangely Lowther is also unusual in that its summit was used as a burial ground for suicide cases who were refused burial in ground consecrated by the church - a rather strange idea to go to so much trouble when there was plenty of much more accessible unconsecrated ground available lower down. There is a tarmacadam road from Green Lowther to Lowther which carries on down all the way to Wanlockhead. I can vouch for its splendid condition as recently I pushed my cycle up Lowther and enjoyed a glorious speedy descent to Wanlockhead with superb views all the way down.

We decided to omit the western top and descend over Cold Moss and Comb Head to the top of the pass where we had left the cycle. I then cycled down to the car and drove up to meet Bill completing an enjoyable outing.

The Queensberry Group

After crossing the Lowther range James IV made his way to Durisdeer and most likely skirted the western slopes of those Donalds to the north-west of Queensberry, grouped around Ballencleuch Law.

Ballencleuch Law, Rodger Law, Comb Law and Shiel Dod

The weather favoured us as it was a very nice sunny afternoon when we drove down from Edinburgh to climb Ballencleuch Law and Comb Law. We drove to the south end of the Daer Reservoir, passed Kirkhope Farm and took to the slopes of Watchman's Brae whence we quickly reached the summit of Rodger Law. It was delightful walking on the lush turf as we made our way to the summit of Ballencleuch Law. Here we retraced our steps for a short way cutting round by Hirtane Rig to Comb Law from which top we then cut down into Kirkhope Cleuch and back to the car. This made another of these delightful afternoon's walking from

The Foot Pilgrimage of James IV to Whithorn

Edinburgh where one is spoiled by the proximity of the lovely Pentlands, Moorfoots and Lammermuirs. The Lowther Hills, however, make a pleasant change and one rarely has to contend with the numbers of walkers one is apt to meet on the more popular ranges.

Shortly after this walk, I found that a new Donald had been nominated, namely Shiel Dod. A return journey was needed and I drove again to Kirkhope Farm and in chatting to the farmer's wife was told that a good sheep track went up the Carsehope Burn and following the first tributary to that burn would lead me easily to the top of Shiel Dod. I followed her advice but came down over Ewe Gair, appropriately named indeed judging by the number of sheep on it, back to the car, deliberately keeping to the ridge to obtain fine views along the Daer reservoir. The ascent was not only enjoyable on its own but it enabled me to get some great views of the many Donalds I had recently been climbing ranging from Queensberry in the south, the nearby Lowthers and, in the distance, Hart Fell and White Coomb.

The Continuation to Whithorn

James continued to Dalry, Penningham and Wigtown to reach his objective at Whithorn. In this part of his journey he would pass close to the Fleet Donalds and to Millfore but I have associated these hills with St. Ninian and with the great Royal Progress in 1563 of James IV's granddaughter, Mary Queen of Scots.

Ben Arthur – The Cobbler

The Royal Progress of Mary, Queen of Scots in 1563

In 1561, Mary returned to Scotland as Queen at the age of nineteen after the death of her husband Francis II, King of France. She was a staunch Roman Catholic but did not interfere with the strongly entrenched Scottish reformed church in the early days of her reign. On the contrary she felt that the Catholic Northern Earls, headed by the Earl of Huntly, had become too strong. Indeed, Mary adopted the advice of her Protestant half-brother, Lord James Stewart, and tried, while retaining her personal religious beliefs, to remain impartial as regards the religious practices of the Scottish nation.

The political story of Mary's reign is all too well known but less is known of the early days of her reign when she, like her predecessors, made a series of Royal Progresses, no doubt with the intention of making herself known to her people. In the course of these Progresses Mary passed close to many Corbetts and Donalds.

The impression conveyed by descriptions of her activities in the early years of her reign is that Mary's interests were, not unnaturally for an attractive young woman in her early twenties, in the pleasures of dancing and music, in hunting and undoubtedly in the male sex. But she did not neglect her monarchial duties and she is recorded as attending councils, opening Parliaments and in attending justicial ayres all over the kingdom in the course of her Progresses

The 1563 Royal Progress
Edinburgh to Inverary Castle

In 1563 she undertook a really ambitious Royal Progress lasting over two months. From Edinburgh she proceeded west by Linlithgow Palace to Glasgow and on to Dumbarton Castle. From there her route took her up Loch Lomond and over 'Rest and Be Thankful' with it's surrounding group of Corbetts and down to the head of Loch Fyne to Inverary Castle. In so doing she would see most of the Munros and all of the Corbetts included in the group called the 'Arrochar Alps'. (*Map 16*)

The Arrochar Alps

Probably the first of the Corbetts to catch her attention would be the famous **Cobbler, or Ben Arthur** to give it it's Corbett name. It is a little sad that this great hill just fails to be a Munro because it is not quite 3000 feet. On all other counts it would well deserve that status.

Ben Arthur (The Cobbler)

I had climbed this peak in my prewar days using Arrochar Hostel before the 'modern' Ardgartan Hostel was opened. I revisited the Cobbler with my grandson, Hamish who was more interested in the Munros, Ben Narnain and Ben Ime. I managed to accompany him to the top of Ben Narnain passing the Narnain Boulders again and looking up at the Cobbler with pleasure.

Beinn Luibhean

This hill is possibly the nearest that Queen Mary came to climbing a Corbett. Her grandfather James IV must have had several Donalds to his credit but her descendant Queen Victoria probably heads the monarchal list with Munros and Corbetts.

The reason for Mary's nearness is that the road at the 'Rest and Be Thankful' pass gives one a lot of height towards the summit of Beinn Luibhean. This was a hill I climbed one day as I was passing . The Arrochar Hills were all in mist as I reached the summit of the pass but I set off directly up a very steep slope. Using compass all the way I quickly reached the summit and must have been too early for the meteorologists as the forecast good weather had not appeared by the time I had made the easy descent back to the car.

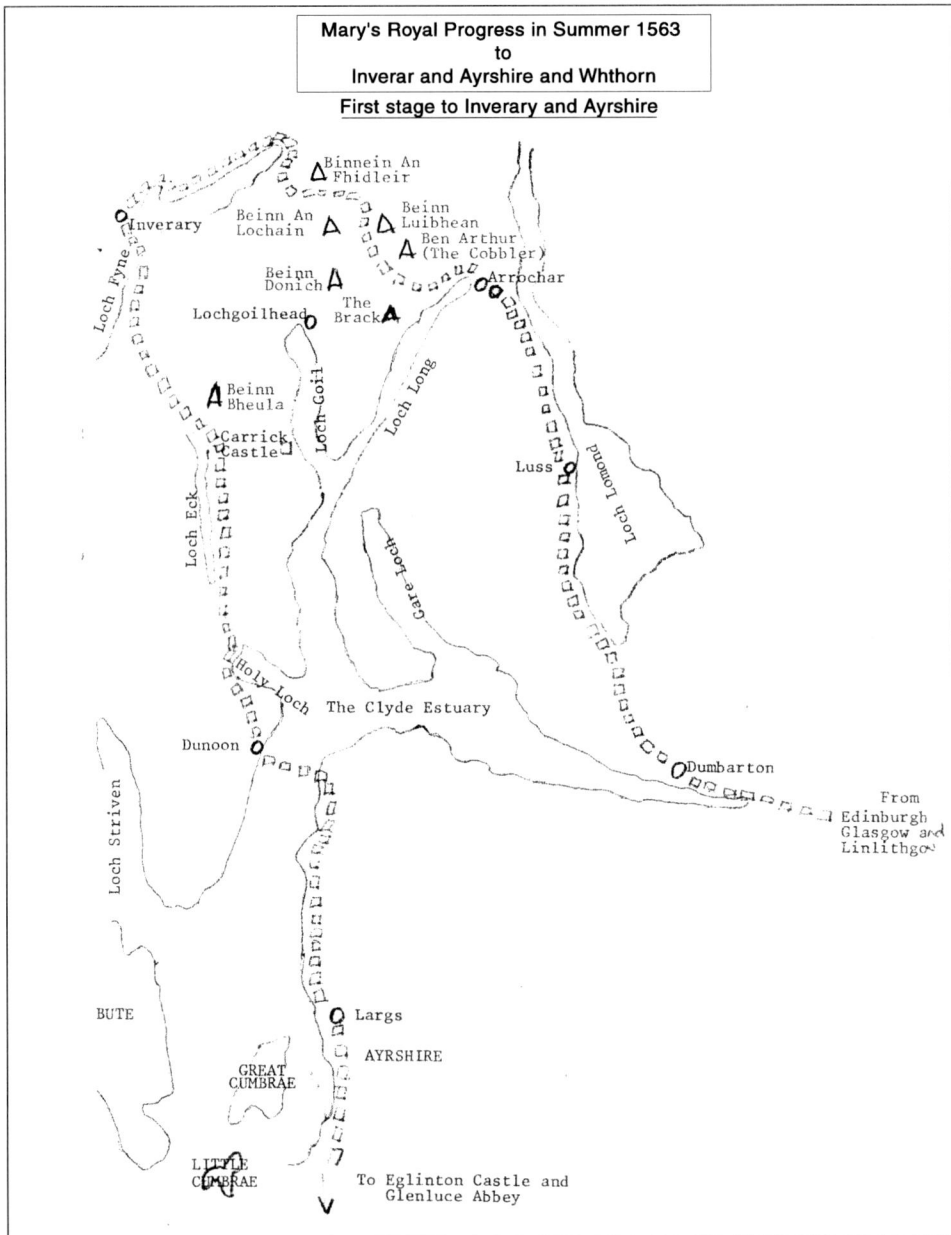

Map 16

Beinn Donich and The Brack

From 'Rest and Be Thankful' I turned down Glen Mhor to the bealach just below Beinn an Lochain where I parked the car. There was a great deal more forestry than was shown on my aged map but I found a firebreak through the forest reaching the top of Beinn Donich with no difficulty . The visibility was a little limited but from time to time I got splendid views of the other 'Alps' including The Brack which I was aiming for. The ridge down to the bealach between Beinn Donich and The Brack involved some rough going but I soon reached the summit cairn of The Brack. I had planned rather carelessly to descend to the main road from the summit of The Brack and walk back up Glen Croe to my car. As I descended I got below the mist and was

The Brack

able to see that there was no suitable bridge over the River Croe. However I could see a well made forest road below me so I descended through some rough old forestry ground to this road and found that it conveniently led me back to my car.

Beinn an Lochain

This hill is for me very much a pre-war Corbett. It was listed in these days as a Munro and has only been reclassified in recent years by the careful revising committees of the Scottish Mountaineering Club.

One New Year a group of us set off to spend a couple of nights in Ardgartan Hostel, then recently opened, and hoped that the weather would allow us to climb Beinn an Lochain. It is sad to think that only three of that happy young group survived the war. In these days of our youth we had little thought of war or arthritis and even less of finesse. We never gave a thought to the interesting north-east ridge of the hill. From the south end of Loch Restil we aimed directly at the south top of the hill. I can still recall the steepness of the slope and numerous little crags to be surmounted on the way up. From the south top it was fairly easy to walk along to the main summit. My main recollection of the summit ridge is the entertainment we had in sliding on a number of small lochans which had frozen over at that height.

Binnien an Fhidhleir (now renamed Stob Coire Creagach)

Early in December I thought that there would be enough daylight for me to travel to the Arrochar area climb Binnien an Fhidhleir and get back to Edinburgh in one day. This was achieved with little difficulty and indeed after the Binnein climb there was time to take a run down to Loch Goil and have a pleasant walk along to Carrick Castle.

For the hill climb I travelled over by 'Rest and Be Thankful' and parked in Glen Kinglas. We set off alongside the stream from the bridge over the Kinglas Water and faced up to a long steep climb (about 2000 feet in under one mile) and reached the Corbett summit in about two hours. We descended along the ridge to the small ruined bothy in the Kinglas Water valley. This bothy has always attracted me because of its unusual name, Abyssinia, and it is only recently that I read the explanation. At one time it was occupied, by an ex- soldier probably, who had visited Abyssinia in the course of his service and so bored his friends with his anecdotes about his time in Abyssinia that eventually they called his house Abyssinia. Rennie McOwan states that this was one of the many pieces of Highland lore collected by Seton Gordon

Inverary Castle to the Ayrshire Coast

From Inverary Queen Mary crossed Loch Fyne and traversed Cowal, probably by Loch Eck, and **Beinn Bheula** nearby to reach Dunoon where she crossed the Firth of Clyde.

Beinn Bheula

It was a lovely day of sunshine when we motored down from 'Rest and Be Thankful' through the beautifully wooded Gleann Mor with the River Goil alongside and the massive slopes of Ben Donich dominating the eastern slopes. At Lochgoilhead, where the Donich Water joins the River Goil before entering Loch Goil, we took the west road alongside Loch Goil leading to Carrick. At Carrick there is the imposing ruined castle built on a promontory, reputed to have been captured by Cromwell's troops in 1651. It was originally the seat of the Lamont family but later became a royal hunting lodge with a Campbell as hereditary keeper.

Our intention had been to park at Cuilmuich and ascend directly to the summit via Cnoc na Tricriche. We parked beside the Carrick Burn but were tempted to follow the new farm road up the north side of the burn rather than tackle the Cnoc head on. Although this may have been a longer way round it soon led us to the ridge and we enjoyed some mild scrambling on the rocky south side of Ben Bheula before reaching the summit.

For me this is a prime candidate for the 'Lochs View' title among the

Corbetts. In addition to tiny Lochan nan Cnaimh rippling and glittering in the sun we could see Loch Fyne, Loch Eck, Loch Goil, Loch Long and possibly a bit of Gareloch and Holy Loch as well as the Firth itself. The magnificent Cobbler took one's eye also and my old favourites Ben Voirlich and Stuc a Chroin could just be picked out. We descended directly over the Cnoc enjoying a little scrambling as we went down. My English companion, Terry, greatly enjoyed his first incursion into this part of Britain but we were both rather surprised at the width and strong construction of the road alongside the Carrick Burn. We later heard that it had been constructed with money available from the European Economic Community which had been allocated to this area. We wondered what the economic arguments in its favour had been.

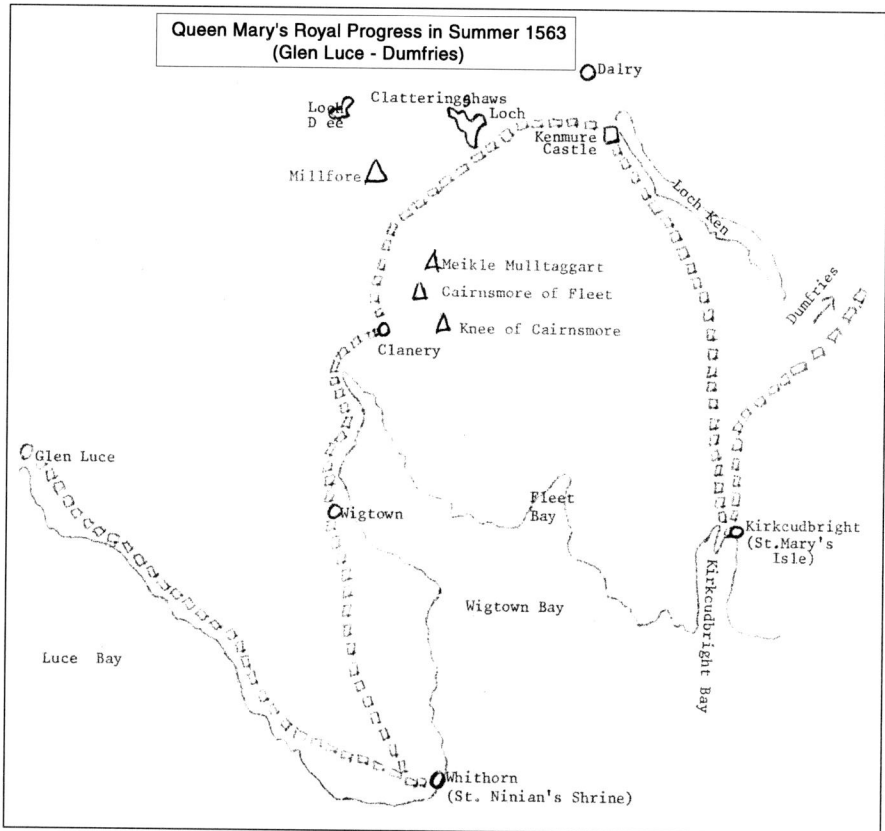

Map 17

Ayrshire, Whithorn to Peebles

Queen Mary proceeded down the Ayrshire coast by Eglinton Castle and Ayr to Glenluce where she resided in the Abbey, as her grandfather James IV had also done (*Map 17*). An even more remote ancestor had also been there; none other than Robert the Bruce.

From there she continued to Whithorn Priory where she turned north up to Clanery near Creetown on the slopes of the Cairnsmore of Fleet Hills. Her next stop was at Kenmure Castle near New Galloway. On this road she would pass close to the slopes of the Donald, **Millfore**. Then she progressed south to Kirkcudbright and Dumfries. From Drumlanrig Castle, her next stop, she took the Mennock Pass to Crawfordjohn. On the east side of the pass the slopes of **East Mount Lowther** come down to the roadside. (*Map 18*) She stayed in Couthalley Castle near Carstairs, then Skirling Castle and on to Peebles.

Millfore

There are quite a number of historical associations with this hill. It was near here, that, in the time of Malcolm IV , the Celtic claimant to the throne Malcolm McHeth was captured. In his foot pilgrimage to St. Ninian's shrine James IV must have passed nearby and the same applies to the other Scottish monarchs who paid visits to the shrine. In this Royal Progress , Queen Mary must also have been near the hill and I have associated Millfore with that Progress.

It is a Donald rather out on its own and I had not been able to fit it in with any other group. So Sandy, Murray and I decided that we could have a day down in the area and get it off our chests en route to the Merrick range walk the next day.

We decided to start from Murray's Monument where there is a convenient parking place. Murray was a local shepherd's son who had a remarkable ability to learn a language and at a very young age became the Professor of Oriental Languages at Edinburgh University. Sadly he died shortly after taking up his post. The King, George III, is reputed to have received a letter from the Emperor of Ethiopa written in his own language and no one could translate it until someone thought of Murray who it turned out, could not only translate it, but could also speak the language. What an asset his abilities would have been in a United Nations post to-day.

We set off up the Grey Mare's Tail Burn and, unfortunately, we followed the burn all the way through rather thick forestry shrubland. We would have had much easier going if we had cut along to the Black Loch by which route we later returned to the car. However we eventually penetrated the thick belt of shrubbery and came to a line of pylons which we followed along until we struck the road coming up from the Black Loch. We continued up until we reached the south east ridge of Millfore and took this all the way to the summit. I had intended to climb the south top of the hill which is listed in the List of Donalds and tops, but we had been held up much longer than we expected by the rough going at the outset. As it was also rather hazy for viewing we turned at the summit and came down by the Black Loch.

East Mount Lowther

After a walk at the Devil's Beef Tub, I drove round to the Mennock Pass and took to the hillside north west of East Mount Lowther. *(Map 18)* Although I had not accurately pin-pointed my starting point, it was a fine enough day for me to see the whole Lowther group and I soon made my way to the top of East Mount Lowther or Auchenlone as it is named on the indicator on the summit. There is certainly a splendid view in all directions but although the indicator refers to Ben More, Ben Lomond, the Paps of Jura and Scafell in England it was just too hazy in the long distance for these far away points to be picked up.

Peebles to Edinburgh via Borthwick Castle

From Peebles, the Queen would most likely take the road along to Innerleithen and then turn up the Leithen Water valley.*(Map 18)* On her right she would pass **Windlestraw Law**, the highest of **the Moorfoot Hills** and on her left, Whitehope Law and Blackhope Scar. She rested for the night at Borthwick Castle. Finally she reached home via Dalhousie Castle and Roslin. It was a truly remarkable progress.

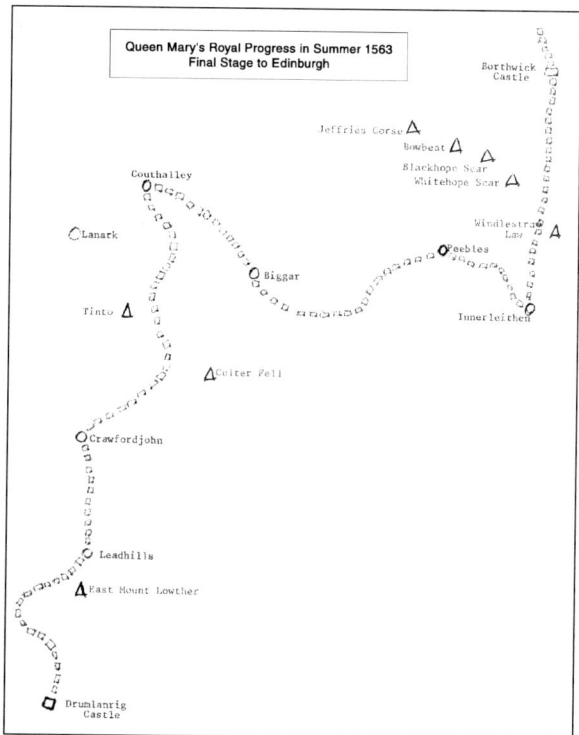

Map 18

The Moorfoot Hills

How fortunate the residents of Edinburgh are to have such splendid walking country within easy reach of the capital city. One of the most satisfying walks is the crossing of the Moorfoot Hills.

It was at the western end of this range that, nearly two centuries after Queen Mary's Progress, Prince Charles' main division passed en route to the invasion of England. They had come by Auchendinny to Leadburn and on to Peebles while the diversionary section under the Prince himself had gone to Kelso. In her extensive Royal Progress Mary passed directly through the Moorfoots on her way from Innerleithen to Borthwick Castle.

It was a fairly bright day when we parked one car at Gladhouse Reservoir and took the second car round by Rosebery Reservoir and Middleton to the Leithen Water road where we parked it at Whitehope Farm beside a colourfully displaying turkey cock. A road led up the east side of the burn and Whitehope Law was reached one hour later. We then continued along the ridge through clumpy heather and slippy snow patches, via Middle Hill to reach the Peebles – Midlothian boundary fence. Here we turned north west over that strikingly named hill, Garvald Punks, to Blackhope Scar. With snow all around us, it was bitterly cold. We continued along the range via Emly Bank to Bowbeat Hill from which there was a somewhat rough crossing to Jeffries Corse. From the summit we selected a descent down a good hill path to Gladhouse Cottage passing the ruined Hirendean Castle, continuing along the road to Moorfoot Farm and then on to the car. Although the visibility had been disappointing for long distance viewing, we had been lucky in having a sufficiently cold day to give us firm ground for crossing several boggy patches.

On the east side of the Leithen Water road is Windelstraw Law, possibly the highest point of the Moorfoots. One crisp cold day I decided to complete the Moorfoot group and at Blackhopebyre Burn walked up to the main summit of Windlestraw. The views of the Eildons and the Cheviots were magnificent. I descended by Bareback Knowe and Dod Hill to the Glentress Water making a good circular walk. Navigation presents little difficulty as there is a good wire fence along the summit ridge.

The parallel roads of Glen Roy and Beinn Iaruinn

Montrose and his Campaign for the Royalists

It is not my purpose to relate all the activities of Montrose, firstly as a strong supporter of the Covenanters and his gradual growing disaffection with his fellow supporters and eventual transfer to support King Charles I, and later on, his son Charles II. My main interest is in his wonderful marches over some of the wildest parts of Scotland's mountainous regions during which his armies must have either traversed the slopes of, or passed close by, many of the Corbetts which I have climbed.

His campaign against the Covenanters began with his arrival at Blair Castle as the King's appointed Lieutenant-General for Scotland. He found Alisdair Macdonald with his group of Irish troops from Antrim and the men of the Atholl clan assembled. They were in the course of an altercation but as he was constantly to show in the ensuing campaign, he had the ability to smooth over differences. In the course of twenty four hours he had decided on the strategy to follow and the campaign started in August 1644.

Montrose and his Campaign for the Royalists

Historians differ as to the value of his campaigns but there is general agreement that he had great tactical skill and that he really fought his battles extraordinarily well bearing in mind that undisciplined Highland clans formed much of his army - clansmen who took their orders from their own chief rather than their General. This must have made it very difficult to plan ahead with any certainty.

Montrose's famous marches in the ensuing twelve months or so, can be grouped into about eight distinct phases, some of them starting and ending at Blair Castle which he maintained as his headquarters during the year. It was here that he held all the important Covenanter prisoners who formed a type of insurance against ill-treatment or execution of the corresponding Royalist prisoners held by the Covenanters.

These numerous marches made by Montrose and his troops are most interesting and many Corbetts were traversed in their course. However there is no doubt in my mind that the most outstanding march was that from Inverary in wintry conditions culminating in the defeat of the Campbells outside Fort William.(*Map 19*) I have therefore confined myself to this magnificent march.

Because of lack of support, Montrose dared not remain a stationary target at Inverary while his enemies geared themselves up for a spring offensive. He therefore decided to make for Inverness. From Inverary, he struck up Glen Aray to Dalmally and then through the Pass of Brander to Loch Etive. After some difficulty he succeeded in ferrying his army over the narrows at Connel under the threat of a sortie from Dunstaffnage Castle nearby. The army then marched into the friendly Stewart of Appin country where indeed they received some modest but encouraging recruitment. Passing on the east Corbetts **Creach Beinn** and **Fraochaidh**, the army marched up through Glencoe. The route possibly passed **Beinn a' Chrulaiste** and **Garbh Bheinn** above Kinlochleven before cutting across some wild country to Loch Eilde Mor with its associated Corbett **Glas Bheinn**. Skirting Corbett **Leum Ulleim** they then marched alongside Loch Treig until they reached Tulloch where the recently promoted Corbett to Munro, Beinn Teallach, can be seen. Then a relatively easy march took them along to Fort Augustus or Kilcummin as it was then known.

Montrose and his Campaign for the Royalists

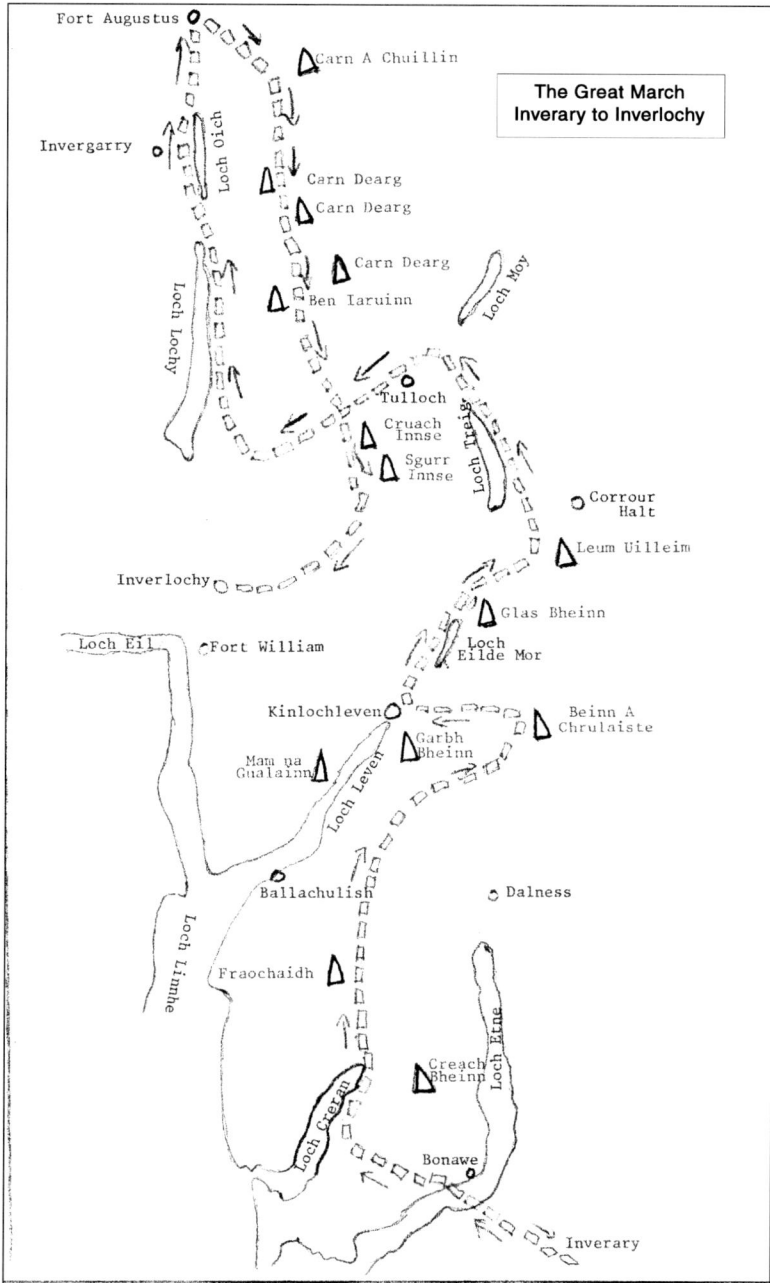

The Great March
Inverary to Inverlochy

Map 19

The Appin Hills
Creach Beinn

Creach Beinn is in Forestry Commission country and as it was the stalking season, I checked with the Oban office that it would be in order to climb the hill. It turned out that the hill was clear of shooting activities that day.

It seemed suitable to start for Creach Beinn at the old railway bridge on Loch Creran. However there was no obvious route up onto the ridge from the Dallachoilish farm there. The farmer's wife suggested that a track, further along the road, would lead us through the thick forest. We found this forest track which certainly took us well up the hill side but it doubled back towards the farm away from the top. We left the road and cut up south through a very much overgrown fire-break and eventually reached the open ridge. Thereafter there was no problem from woods but there were numerous ups and downs and there were at least three steps before the subsidiary top, east of Meall Garbh, was reached. From there a change of direction to south-west took us to the summit in about half a mile. On the way down, we could not find where we had come through the forest on the way up and had a laborious crash through the trees before we came to the forest road we had used. We felt certain that this could not be the best line of ascent and descent.

Fraochaidh

Fraochaidh was approached on a day of beautiful sunshine. I had ascertained that I could drive my car quite a way up Glen Duror. I noticed a bridge over the River Duror and there seemed to be a good track wending its way up through the tree-covered hill-side. I followed the track but it started to descend and I had to force a way through the forest until I eventually reached the open ridge. From the long summit ridge there are superb views. The Beinn a Bheithir group stood out particularly well with Aonach Eagach in the background and the Loch Creran Munros were splendid.

For the descent, I thought I could improve on my ascent route as there seemed to be a fire break in Coire Dubh but this proved to be very rough and it needed a lot of pushing and scrambling before I got clear of the forest.

Glencoe
Beinn a'Chrulaiste

Beinn a'Chrulaiste was one of the Corbetts which I had set aside as being a possibility for climbing as I was passing through. This indeed proved easily possible but it should not be allowed to detract from the status of the hill as a viewpoint. It is superbly placed as such. Having ascended the east ridge of the hill from the Kingshouse Hotel side-road in splendid weather, I soon attained the summit and as with so many Corbetts, it proved the superb viewpoint I was expecting. The Glencoe hills, the Blackmount Hills the Mamores and the Ben Nevis area were magnificently displayed. It was with reluctance that I descended to my car in the gloaming.

Garbh Bheinn and Mam na Gualainn

As the march continued up Glencoe it probably crossed over to Kinlochleven by the Devil's Staircase before pushing on to Loch Eilde Mhor. I had chosen Kinlochleven as a suitable base for three Corbetts - Garbh Bheinn, Mam na Gualainn and Glas Bheinn allowing myself two days to do the three.

From Kinlochleven, I drove along to Caolasnacoan whence I struck up the obvious north-east ridge of Garbh Bheinn. It was a ridge with a number of bumps on it and as often happens, I was tempted by an inviting grassy slope to try to traverse round some of the bumps. However this was not a good idea as I found myself on the steep and stony south-west side of the hill and it took much longer to reach the summit than the straightforward ascent of the ridge would have done.

As the situation of the hill suggests, the views of Aonach Eagach and the Mamores were outstanding. I took the straightforward route in descent and enjoyed a good walk down with the waters of Loch Leven glistening in the mid-day sun. After a leisurely lunch at the water side I proceeded round to Mam na Gualainn which is a bit off the Montrose march but which I combined with Garbh Bheinn. I started from Callert House and a good path took me up to the bealach to the west of the hill. These two hills made a very pleasant day's walking in the fine weather.

Looking over Loch Leven to Mam na Gualainn

Montrose and his Campaign for the Royalists

Glas Bheinn

The Montrose march probably proceeded up towards Mamore Lodge and Loch Eilde Mor. I took my car up to the Lodge where I parked it. As I proceeded towards Loch Eilde Mor I noticed a lot of small flags with SO or L or R on them which I rightly assumed to mean straight on, left and right. I could not see the point of them until later in the day the peaceful scene was 'enlivened', if you like the noise of motor cycle engines, by the competitors in the Pre- 1965 All British motor cycle trial. It was quite a rough track for such old cycles and indeed some of them had trouble.

I crossed the Allt na h' Eilde by the dam and proceeded to Meall na Cruaidhe where I left the flag-decorated track leading the motor cyclists to the Blackwater reservoir. From here it was a straight walk north-east to the summit of Glas Bheinn over somewhat rough ground. Although it was a good walking day and the cloud was high the long distance views were obscure and I did not delay on the summit. I was not sure if there was a bridge over the stream between Loch Eilde Mor and Loch Eilde Beag but my monocular proved its usefulness as it enabled me to pick one out and I descended in that direction and back along the lochside to meet the ascending motor cyclists.

Leum Uilleim

In the descent by Loch Treig to Tulloch Montrose's army would traverse the slopes of Leum Uilleim en route. I had an interesting day on this hill as Sandy and I decided to fit it in between trains from the Corrour Halt by leaving Edinburgh at an appropriately early hour. We had coffee at Crianlarich station and then sat back to enjoy the rail journey through the Bridge of Orchy Munros and Corbetts and the Blackmount hills in the distance before cutting across the moor to Corrour where we left the train.

The path onto the north-east ridge of Beinn a Bhric was easily picked up at a gate beyond the station and we reached Beinn a Bhric inside the time we had allowed to ensure catching the return train. The ridge across to the summit of Leum Uilleim took about half-an-hour and we were then able to enjoy at leisure the Loch Ossian Munros, the Loch Treig group, the Grey corries and the Mamores. It was satisfying too, to identify the Loch Leven Corbetts. The descent to the station was easy and we found that we had ample time to look round to the magnificently sited Loch Ossian hostel.

Battle at Inverlochy

During winter, the Covenanters had been reassembling their troops and Argyll had sent for his battle-experienced clansman, Campbell of Auchenbreck, to lead the Campbell troops. At Fort Augustus, Montrose was initially unaware of the Campbell forces being massed behind him and thought that he had only the McKenzies ahead of him to be tackled. He was preparing to march against them when his scouts let him know that the Campbells, outnumbering him by two to one, were massing at Inverlochy. He immediately decided to turn back and fight them on Highlanders' country rather than be sandwiched between McKenzies and Campbells in the Great Glen at Inverness. (*Map 19*)

Instead of prosaically marching back along the Great Glen, he cut up Glen Tarff skirting the slopes of Corbett **Carn a'Chuilinn** and continued, crossing over the Corrieyairack Pass road by some rough country to the Corbett **Carn Dearg** at the head of Glen Roy. Here he passed the other two **Carn Dearg** Corbetts in Glen Roy as well as **Beinn Iaruinn** getting some shelter in the glen from the wintry conditions. Unexpectedly a Campbell scouting party was encountered at Keppoch and the Royalist army had to move with care in order not to arouse the Campbells. Montrose led his troops over the River Spean, not far from Corbetts Cruach Innse and Sgurr Innse, along the Cour Burn. Skirting the slopes of the Ben Nevis massif, they took up position in the evening darkness above Inverlochy. Here they were discovered by another small Campbell scouting party who reported their presence to Argyll and Auchenbreck. Auchenbreck could not credit that Montrose had brought his whole army across the hills in such adverse conditions and decided merely to double his guards and treat the Royalists as a raiding party. Great was the astonishment in the morning when the Royalist forces were observed drawn up on the slopes above them. Argyll took to his galley once again as a precaution. Auchenbreck and his men faced the charge of the Highlanders down the hillside. The Lowland regiments with him broke before the charge but the Campbells under his command fought firmly and Auchenbreck was killed in the action. The Covenanters fled along the shores of Loch Linnhe and Loch Eil and more slaughter took place there rather than on the battlefield. Argyll sailed away in his galley to fight another day.

This battle was possibly the highlight of Montrose's year of campaigns. One of the by- products was the conversion of the MacKenzies, the Grants and some of the Gordons to the Royalist cause - a decision which could possibly have had a degree of self interest in it. But Montrose was still no nearer achieving his strategic objective of joining up with the King's forces in North England. He did, however, help the Royal cause there indirectly as some of the Scottish Covenanting forces in England were withdrawn to Perth to help to deal with the threat caused by his campaign.

Carn a'Chuilinn

The return route up Glen Tarff crossed the lower slopes of Carn a'Chuilinn which I approached from the Glen Doe side. This was one of the occasions when my old map was inadequate for the purpose required as there had been a new road introduced since the 1941 survey. We were lucky enough to meet a stalker who gave us a route to follow. Even so we went too far west and went much further round than was necessary eventually reaching the summit along a long ridge south of Carn Doire Chaorach. It was very cold on top but the visibility was good and we thought we could identify many of the Cluanie, the Monar and Cannich groups. We were able to descend by the direct way back to our car.

Glen Roy
The Three Carn Deargs and Beinn Iaruinn

The army crossed the very rough country through the Culachy Forest crossing over the Corrieyairick Pass road to the heart of Glen Roy where the slopes of the northern of the three Carn Dearg Corbetts of Glen Roy are situated.

Starting from Roy Bridge we motored up Glen Roy getting splendid views of the parallel roads as we passed. Crossing by the Turret Bridge we took the ridge going up between the Roy and the Turret onto the slopes of Carn Dearg Beag. From here it was easy walking to reach the middle Carn Dearg Corbett where we sheltered from the cold wind. Heavy snow and thick mist then befell us and it was not so pleasant going on to the northern Carn Dearg. The mist and snow continued all the way down to Glen Turret where it cleared enabling us to have a fine walk back to the lodge amid large numbers of sheep and early lambs. From the middle Carn Dearg we had views of Ben Nevis and the Loch Lochy hills and could pick out the 'window' on Creag Meagaidh.

Conditions were much less severe when I returned two months later to climb the southern Carn Dearg and Beinn Iaruinn. I had at one time thought I would like to climb all three Carn Deargs in the one outing but the snow conditions had blocked me on the previous occasion and so as a compromise I set out to climb the southern Carn Dearg and Beinn Iaruinn on the same day.

I crossed the River Roy at the bridge above Brunachan, (where there is now a Mountain Bothy) and struck up the slopes of Carn Brunachain. I met the shepherd who was busy gathering in his sheep and lambs. He told me that I would have been better to have followed up Coire na Reinich and at the top bear south west to the summit. However it was probably much easier to descend over the tops. He expressed surprise that a person of my age was intending to climb Beinn Iaruinn when I got down. If I did, he recommended ascent by the south side of the Allt Dearg rather than going up the steep west end of the hill which looked an interesting climb. I took his advice and although the slope was somewhat steep in parts the going was good and I quickly reached the ridge. Although it was a long walk along the ridge to the summit it was a most enjoyable one as the views all round were outstanding. I thought that I could pick out Ben Hope away to the north, the Fannich hills, the Glen Shiel Hills, Ardgour and Skye beyond and Sgur na Ciche and the Knoydart hills. To the south the two Innses were shining in the sun. I have allocated these two Corbetts to the Fifteen Rising.

Meall na Leitreach and Dalnaspidal

General Monck's Campaign

Charles II in Scotland and Cromwell in England

After the execution of Charles I, both Scotland and Ireland had accepted the succession of Charles II but Cromwell in England soon established a Protectorate. Cromwell quickly defeated the Irish and Charles II had to rely on the Scottish leaders to support his attempt at restoration of his throne. Those leaders were quite bigoted in their support for the Solemn League and Covenant. They insisted that before they would back him for the throne Charles must accept the principles of the Covenant. Charles reluctantly accepted the ecclesiastical terms, but his acceptance was effectively under coercion. These negotiations coloured his views in his future dealings with the Scottish nation. After the Restoration he never returned to Scotland.

General Monck's Campaign

However, in 1650, Charles II landed at Speymouth. Cromwell at once reacted by invading Scotland, and crossing the Tweed installed himself near Dunbar. Here he was hemmed in by Leslie and the Scottish army. But, possibly under pressure from the church leaders, Leslie abandoned his strong position and attacked. He was heavily defeated. In an attempt to relieve the strain, Charles and his army marched into England and, as the King had hoped, Cromwell turned and pursued him. But the Royalist army was defeated at Worcester. Charles, after many adventures, fled to the continent.

Cromwell had left behind him in Scotland a force commanded by General Monck and this force captured the Scottish government leaders who were sitting at Alyth. Although strong pockets of resistance still held out, particularly in the north, the country was without a government and without a strong army after the defeat at Worcester. Monck was therefore free to deal with the remaining opposition as he wished.

In early 1652, a political union of the two countries was planned by Cromwell in which there was to be a nominal Scottish representation in the British parliament. On the military front in Scotland, however, Monck proceeded with his plans. On the continent, in mid-1652, war broke out between England and Holland, and Charles, hoping for aid from the Dutch , proceeded to appoint Middleton as his Commander – in – Chief in Scotland. This, however, did not keep Cromwell from proceeding with his political plans. In 1653, a political union between the two countries was proclaimed. This proclamation converted the smouldering discontent in Scotland into active opposition and in July 1653, Glencairn's uprising commenced.

While Middleton was still on the continent, Charles had appointed the Earl of Glencairn to be his commander in Scotland. Although Glencairn's rising gradually gained support in the Lowlands, it never became a cohesive whole and remained a group of separate efforts. This suited the ideas of General Monck completely and his successful campaign resulted in subjugation of the whole country

The Campaign 1653 – 1655

Monck's general strategy was to establish a series of strong points with the objective of splitting the Royalist forces into smaller groups which could be dealt with separately. He was particularly anxious to seal off the Lowlands from the Highlands. The principal Highland strong points were to be Perth, Ruthven Barracks at Kingussie, Inverness and Fort William. In the Lowlands he established his Headquarters at Dalkeith and in early 1654 marched to Stirling,and went on to Perth. His strong points at Inverness, Inverlochy and Ruthven were already established so he decided to proceed with the next phase of his campaign from Perth.

The March to Ruthven Barracks

From Perth, Monck marched along Loch Tay, occupied Weems Castle and Garth Castle and captured Kenmore. Here his scouts advised him of a Royalist rendezvous near Loch Ness and he therefore decided to march for Ruthven. From Kenmore he crossed into Glen Lyon, over by Coshieville to Loch Rannoch, up by Glen Errochty, traversing the slopes of **Beinn a'Chuallaich**, to Dalnacardoch. From there he took the Gaick pass road by the now ruined Sronphadruig Lodge and Loch an Duin with its guardian Corbetts, **An Dun** and **Maol Creag an Loch**, past Gaick Lodge and Loch an't Seilich and down Glen Tromie to cross over by Glen Tromie Lodge to the barracks.

Beinn a'Chuallaich

Even in the time of General Monck the crossing from Loch Rannoch to Dalnacardoch would probably be well delineated. Beinn a'Chuallaich, over whose slopes Monck's men passed en route for Ruthven, was, for me, a particularly enjoyable Corbett as it had been selected by my friends Frances and Munro to be their joint final Corbett. I was very pleased to be one of the happy party who had been invited to celebrate the occasion. Frances and Munro had nominated a point on the Trinafour road for the meeting place to start from and we proceeded up a path along to the ridge reaching the Meall nan Eun end of the summit ridge via Loch na Caillich, where my dog Tom greatly enjoyed swimming all around the loch. The top was reached comfortably by the variety of age groups from geriatric to paediatric, with baby Megan having the most comfortable ascent on her parent's back. However she did not share the champagne and cake which the rest of us enjoyed! The views of the nearby tops were splendid as, from here, Schiehallion and Farragon are most shapely hills.

An Dun and Creag an Loch
(Creag an Loch is now named Maol Creag an Loch.)

From Dalnacardoch Sandy and I followed the old Gaick pass route on our cycles and in due course reached the now ruined lodge of Sronphadruig. Passing the wood behind the lodge buildings, we decided to go to the small bealach immediately to the east of the lodge and then north-east along the fine ridge overlooking Loch an Duin. At the Perth-Inverness border line we followed an east bearing to reach the two summit points of the hill. From the summit a west bearing was taken leading to a very sharp descent at the north end of Loch an Duin. We had no trouble in fording the Allt Loch an Duin and then faced an equally sharp ascent to the summit of An Dun. The visibility was hazy and we had no inducement to tarry but found a relatively easy route back to the lodge. The special treat of the day was the sight of a mother ptarmigan and her seven chicks, orange yellow in colour. It was a joy to see how well she protected them.

The Chase to Kintail

When Monck reached Ruthven Barracks, he found that Middleton, the Royalist General, had by now come over from the continent, and taken over from the Earl of Glencairn. He had split his forces and was sending the infantry to Kintail to sail to Skye and was sending the cavalry to Lochaber. Monck then carried out a series of long marches with his army. He left Kingussie not far from Corbett **Carn an Fhreiceadain**, and marched to Cluny Castle, then to Glen Roy, and, after a night's rest, on to Fort William. From here they turned up the Great Glen where they met the Marquis of Argyll, professing to be a supporter of the General, at the head of Loch Lochy. Still taking the view that Middleton and his troops were in the Kintail area, Monck led his men from Fort Augustus over to Glen Moriston, using the old Military road through Inchnacardoch Forest to Achclain in Glen Moriston. (*Map 20)* On his left were the slopes of Corbett **Meall Dubh.** In Glen Moriston, his scouts assured him that Middleton was still in Kintail. So Monck proceeded down Glen Sheil passing between Corbetts **Druim nan Cnamh** on his left and **Am Bathach** on his right. With the main force Monck continued to Loch Alsh passing the slopes of Sgurr an Airgid but, as there had been reports that Middleton was going over to Skye, he also sent a subsidiary force over Mam Ratagan and the slopes of the Corbett, **Sgurr Mhic Bharraich**, to Glenelg. However, his information was faulty and Middleton had moved on. Monck thought that he must have turned north. In fact Middleton had not done so but had marched down into the heart of the Highlands.

Monck at this stage decided to return to Inverness and marched his army up the side of Loch Long into Glen Ling over the northern slopes of the **Ben Killilan – Sguman Coinntich massif, Aonach Buidhe, Faochaig** and **Beinn Dronaig**. At the summit of the crossing they would pass Loch Cruoshie, Lochan Dobhlach and Loch an Tachdaidh where the old path led to Patt Lodge and probably down the north side of Loch Monar (which would not have been dammed at that time). In doing so they would traverse the lower slopes of Corbett **An Sidhean.**

Continuing on to Inverness Monck marched his army on into Glen Strathfarrar with Corbett Sgor na Diollaid on the right. Probably they went as far as Struy, near Corbett **Beinn a'Bha 'ach Ard** on the left, into Strath Glass and then down to Glen Urquhart, Loch Ness and along towards the city.

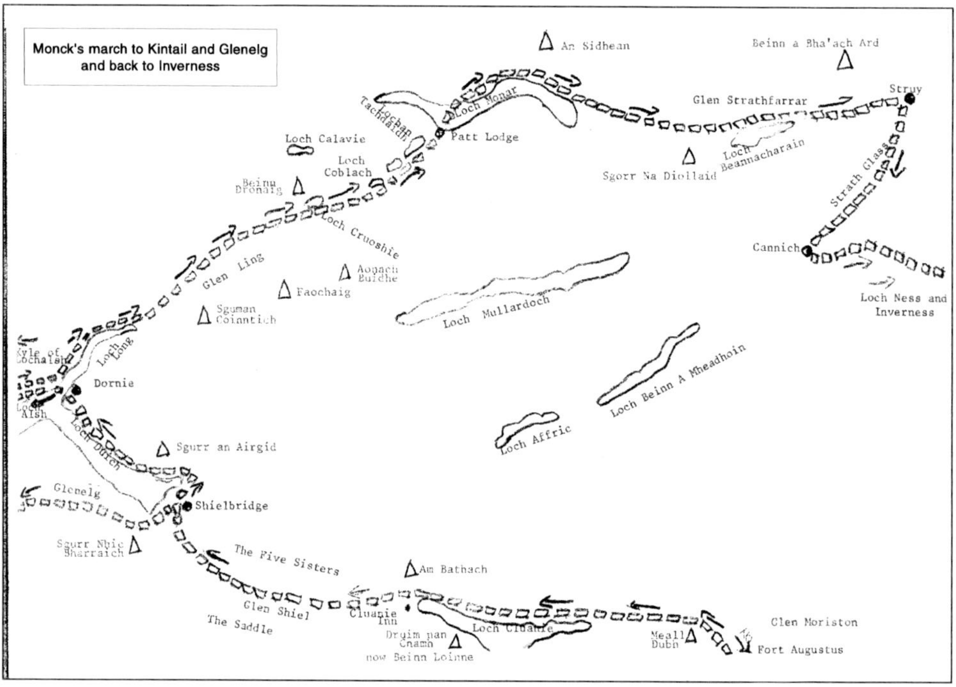

Map 20

Carn an Fhreiceadain

It was a nice sunny morning when we parked the car at the Kingussie golf-course car-park and cycled up the glen along the banks of the Allt Mhor or the Gynack Burn as I knew it. At Pitmain Lodge we left our cycles and followed the east bank intending to cross over to the west bank at the marked ford. But we could not get across the burn and had to continue through some rough ground on the east bank. Finally we ascended the south outlier of Carn an Freiceadain, Meall Unaig, directly to the summit. There was a good deal of snow around and we enjoyed some short glissades on the way down. This was a typical Monadliath hill with some superb views of the Cairngorms as one descends to the car-park. The return along the Allt Mhor is very pleasing on a sunny day.

General Monck's Campaign

_____

Meall Dubh

I made use of the 'new' road over from Invergarry. Quite apart from the objective of Meall Dubh, this is a splendid road for views over the surrounding countryside and I usually contrive to have a coffee stop at one or other of the parking places to enjoy the views of Loch Garry or down Glen Sheil over Loch Loyne. Shapely Ben Tee, one of my favourite Corbetts for shape, stands out superbly. We parked at the 'new' Loch Loyne dam and, skirting an Economic Forestry Group plantation, we steadily ascended over rather rough ground to the summit of the hill. I had been looking forward to the view for this was clearly one of the great Corbett situations. The views down Glen Kingie and down Glenshiel would have been worth lingering over. Sadly, however the mist came down on the way up and the views had to be left to my imagination.

Druim nan Cnamh (now named Beinn Loinne)

Druim nan Cnamh is almost as well sited a Corbett as Meall Dubh. Taken on its own, Druim nan Cnamh is a simple hill to climb as the old Tomdoun road from Cluanie Inn takes one well up towards the summit. This was the way we went, in lovely sunshine, and we walked as far as need be on the old 'Road to the Isles'. As expected the views in all directions were exceptional. The two ridges of Glen Shiel, south and north, closed off by the Saddle were clearly delineated. The A'Chralaig and Conbhairean groups showed up well, and to the south the Glen Quoich forest hills brought back happy memories of nearly sixty years ago.

Am Bathach

I had already tried to climb Am Bathach when I was passing down Strath Cluanie but unfortunately, it was 'occupied' by a deer stalking party. On a fine summer's day however I had a second opportunity and followed a rough stalker's path up the south east slopes by the small wood and soon reached the first of several little 'false' tops. It was a surprisingly narrow grassy ridge along to the main summit for about three quarters of a mile and had I still been doing the Munros the temptation to continue up Ciste Dubh would have been irresistible. However the walk along the ridge gives really superb views of the great Glen Shiel ridges all around and I returned along the ridge for this reason.

Sgurr Mhic Bharraich

The top of the pass, Mam Ratagan, was my starting point and I followed the ridge tops which made for a great deal of up and down work over very rough and craggy ground. Later in the week we had a long talk

95

with the keeper, and although we had gained considerable height by driving up to the top of the Mam Ratagan pass, he thought that we would have found the path up the Allt Undalain leading round to Loch Coire nan Crogachan a much easier line of approach.

Sguman Coinntich

It was a day of snow showers and strong winds with sunny intervals when I took the good stalker's path up the north bank of the Allt a Choire Mhoir almost to the Bealach Mhic Bheathain. Where the path started to diverge from the stream, I went down and as I was sufficiently far up, was eventually able to find a place to cross the stream which was in spate. A steady climb up the steep slopes of the hill took me to the ridge not too far from the summit of Sguman Coinntich. It was only when I stood out on the ridge that I realised the tremendous force of the wind and this provided me with my main recollection of the hill as I was actually blown off my feet. The wind was so troublesome that I had not much inclination to stand and enjoy the view of the snow-covered Strath Carron hills. Although the snow was soft, considerable care was needed in the descent down the steep ridge to the point where I could cross the Allt a'Choire Mhoir.

Faochaig and Aonach Buidhe

I contacted the stalker when I got down to Killilan to see if I could get permission to take my car up to Iron Lodge the next day, but he regretfully told me that the new owners had given him strict orders not to allow cars up the glen. However he suggested that the retired shepherd, Alistair Macrae, who went up the glen each morning to inspect the sheep, would give me a lift up with my folding cycle. This satisfactory arrangement I duly made.

I set off up the An Crom Allt. As I was intending to descend Aonach Buidhe by the south-west ridge on the way back, I ascertained that there was a bridge over the stream on the Loch Mhoicean path. The path led up to the bealach between the hills where I had to cross the stream in spate. There is an old ruin at the bealach which provided some shelter from the gale. About half a mile beyond the ruin, there are two small cairns at the side of the road marking the start of a stalker's path up Faochaig. Although the path is indistinctly marked in places, it is a good one, going all the way onto the summit ridge, where there was a considerable amount of snow. The walk along the ridge to the summit was broad and easy and the task for the next part of the day, Aonach Buidhe, was clearly visible. The views of Sgurr nan Ceathreamhnan and its supporters in snow were particularly fine and I did enjoy seeing this splendid and remote group of Munros from almost a grandstand situation.

General Monck's Campaign

I returned to the ruin before setting off up the west slopes of Aonach Buidhe. The weather was deteriorating and I did not delay on the top but, as planned, took the long south west slope down to the bridge. Despite the strong wind in my face it was a pleasant cycle down the glen to Killilan where I called in to tell Alistair Macrae how I had got on.

Faochaig from Aonach Buidhe

Beinn Dronaig

I had climbed from Attadale using my cycle to take me to Beinn Dronaig Lodge. The path up to Loch Calavie was followed for a short distance before striking up the north slope of the hill and a steady slog took me to the top where again the Bidean and Lurg Mhor dominate the scene. This is a simple climb on its own but it isn't too simple getting there. And, even though it is downhill a lot of the way, it is also a long cycle back. It was however a lovely evening and the views to the north in the evening sun amply compensated for the weariness of the cycle run.

An Sidhean

On the north side of Loch Monar the lower slopes of Corbett An Sidhean would be passed by the Monck columns but they are unlikely to have noticed the Corbett with the other and much fiercer hills surrounding them.

General Monck's Campaign

Since Strath Farrar is now a National Nature Reserve it was necessary for us to pick up permits at Struy to go up the glen. I suppose that permits have something to do with the arrangements made with the private landlords who still own part of the glen. But somehow I feel a sense of illogicality that the institution of public ownership should be accompanied by the institution of permits and limited hours also.

Ever since I first went there, in the thirties, I have considered Strath Farrar to be a glen of outstanding beauty and wildness - both of which characteristics are unchanged to-day. We left our car at the Monar Dam and continued on to the Lodge where we met the shepherd cum stalker. He was very helpful and told us of the excellent path alongside the Loch where, after crossing the third wooden bridge over the Allt na Cois, there is a good pony track leading up to the tops. Although the track is not too easily spotted it leads well on to the Mullach a Gharbh-leathaid ridge. From the ridge it is a straight walk north to the summit. At the top the views were extensive with the Fannichs and An Teallach visible. The nearby hills were splendid in their coating of snow.

Beinn a'Bha'ach Ard

From our base at Boat of Garten, Frances, Munro and I drove to Struy reaching there about 11 a.m. We had intended to drive the car a short distance up Strath Farrar but discovered that the National Nature Reserve did not open till 1.30p.m.; a regulation which served to reinforce my feeling of illogicality about the issue of permits. As it was not far to go we walked up to the Power station and followed the Electricity Board road up to a small cairn where we cut onto the hillside under the pylons. We found a path which led us onto the slopes above Culligran and we then cut across the moorland direct to the summit. As we discovered later it would have made for an easier ascent if we had used the path we took for our descent; a path shown on the west side of the hill along the Neaty Burn. However on the way down, it was a long time before we picked the path up and rejoined the Electricity Board road where we had started. This is not an outstanding Corbett view point but we picked up Ben Wyvis, and faintly the Cairngorms, the Sgurr na Lapaich group and to the east the Black Isle country.

The Engagement at Dalnaspidal

In Inverness Monck met his deputy Colonel Morgan. Monck still thought that Middleton had gone north and so he instructed Morgan to take his forces into Caithness. While at Inverness he found that Middleton had turned south. Morgan was recalled and ordered to return to Ruthven Barracks while Monck himself started in pursuit of Middleton, reported by his scouts to be at Dunkeld making for Loch Lomond.

He marched through Atholl to Weems Castle where he reprovisioned his army. *(Map 21)* He then marched along Loch Tay to Lawers where he discovered that he was only a day's march behind Middleton. Continuing along Glen Dochart into Glen Lochy his scouts made contact with Middleton's forces in Glen Strae, near Corbett Beinn Mhic -Mhonaidh. Monck at once marched on and Middleton's force was caught by surprise and withdrew north in some disarray. One contingent made for Loch Rannoch and the main body made for Badenoch, where, although they did not know it, Morgan and his forces were waiting to intercept them. Monck then turned and continued his march along Strath Fillan at a more leisiurely pace as he considered, rightly, that the Royalist troops were in some disarray and that Morgan was in a strong position to deal with them at Dalnaspidal. The Royalist cavalry was completely routed and the infantry broken up. Monck sent troops across into Glen Lyon to round up stragglers and they continued round the Loch Rannoch area for the same purpose. They scoured the slopes of the three Corbetts **Beinn Pharlagain**,the rather distant **Stob an Aonaich Mhoir**, and **Beinn Mholach**.

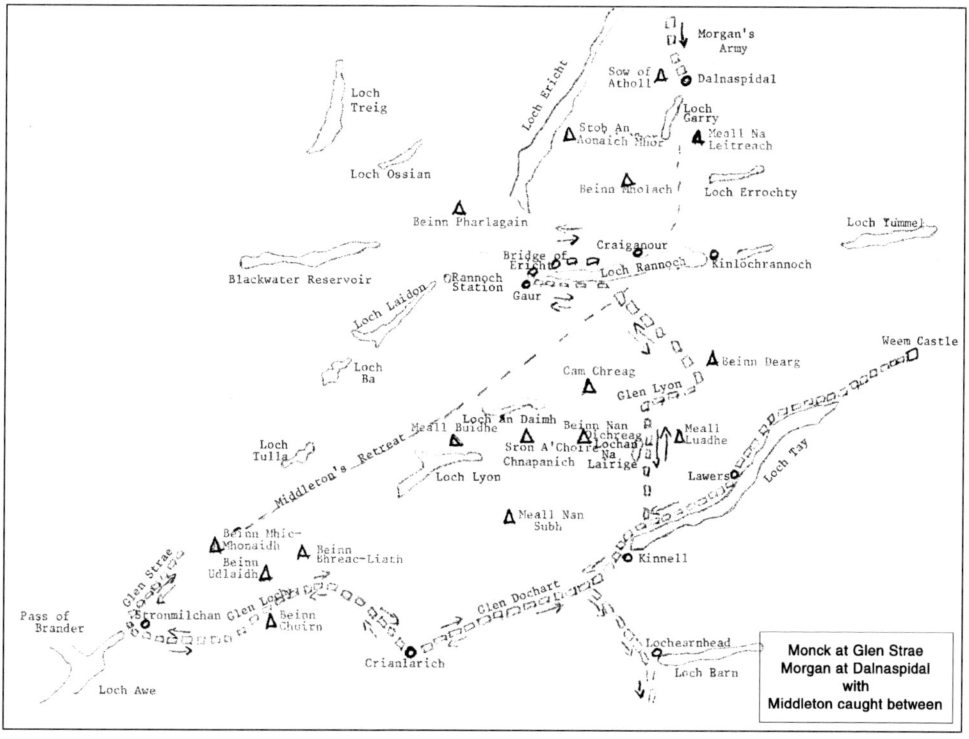

Map 21

General Monck's Campaign

The Loch Rannoch trio of Corbetts
Beinn Pharlagain

Mike and Barbara were contemplating a not too strenuous walk and so I selfishly suggested a Corbett which I had not climbed - Beinn Pharlagain at the west end of Loch Rannoch. This they kindly agreed to even though they were still in the throes of climbing the Munros. As if to reward their forbearance, we had a superb day of sunshine when we set off early from Edinburgh, straight to the west end of Loch Rannoch.

We set off up the track leading to Corrour Old Lodge, and after crossing the Allt Gormag, cut up the south slope of Leacann nan Giomach. On this slope there is a series of these frustrating subsidiary tops each of which, when one gets there, reveals yet another likely looking summit which once again turns out to be another subsidiary top. I counted five of them before we reached the final summit. It was a day for savouring the views and it gave us an extensive panaroma; the Ben Dorain group, the Grey Corries and the Ben Nevis massif, the Loch Treig and Loch Ossian Hills, and away in the distance what must have been ,we thought, Beinn A'ghlo. The descent back down the Corrour Old Lodge path was a delight in the afternoon sunshine and it was fascinating to see the trains crossing the moor, as they looked just like the old Hornby outfits of my youth.

Stob an Aonaich Mhoir

It would be a long trek for Monck's 'clearing up' troops to reach the slopes of this hill, rather distant from Loch Rannoch. There would certainly not be available to them the motor road leading from Ericht Bridge to the dam at the west end of Loch Ericht. At Ericht Bridge we checked with the Keeper's wife who confirmed that there would be no objection to us cycling up the road which also leads to the Coire Bhachdaidh Lodge. The road continues up the glen parallel to the Allt Glas. For a time we were misled by the Carn Dearg summit but there was no doubt about the cairn on the top of Stob an Aonaich Mhor from which a lovely view down Loch Ericht revealed itself. Needless to say, the Ben Alder group dominated the scene and it was nice to see Culra Bothy peeping round the shoulder of Beinn Bheoil with Loch Pattack in the distance.

Beinn Mholach

The gentle south slopes of Beinn Mholach run down over Plucach to Craiganour Lodge on the shores of Loch Rannoch and it was at Craiganour Lodge that we took the tarmacadam road leading up to the well-kept lodge. We then followed the track along the Allt a'Chreagain Odhair until we came to a footbridge enabling us to cross over to follow the track up the

Aulich Burn. This track eventually ran out near a small bothy pin-pointed by two large posts. We took to the hill here and found that a reasonably good hill-track took us to the foot of Beinn Mholach. In beautiful sunshine we reached the summit and enjoyed a view comparable to that from Beinn Pharlagain further west.

The Sow of Atholl and Meall na Leitreach

I had travelled up the A9 to Inverness on innumerable occasions and but had never stopped to climb The Sow although I had climbed 'The Boar' on the way back from a Munro expedition. The Sow is another of these Corbetts which can be climbed 'en passant' and one afternoon, as I drove down the A9, I stopped at Dalnaspidal, crossed the railway and went along the farm road to make use of a bridge over the streams which were in spate. An uneventful steady climb soon took me to the top in misty conditions and I made a simple return back to the same crossing point.

For Meall na Leitreach, Frances, Munro and I picked a sunny February day to climb the snow covered hill. Once again we crossed the swollen streams by the farm bridges. The snow made the going fairly heavy but gave no problems. Loch Garry below was frozen over. With the sun and the snow some interest was introduced into what was otherwise a rather uninspiring climb.

Monck's Military Control of Scotland

The encounter at Dalnaspidal really completely destroyed the Royalist military potential in Scotland although Middleton himself escaped with a small body of troops. Apart from a number of isolated pockets of resistance Monck was virtually in complete control of the country. He therefore returned to Stirling but did not relax in his efforts to deal with the remaining resistance groups. He succeeded in his efforts and gradually the Royalist leaders surrendered. Glencairn himself, Atholl and Montrose all capitulated and Monck gave them remarkably lenient terms albeit with high monetary security for their continued compliance. Eventually, in mid-1655 Middleton gave up the struggle and fled back to the continent.

Monck was now in complete control of Scotland and it must be said that he exercised his powers very ably. In a successful attempt to control the civilian population he involved the local leaders in responsibility for maintenance of law and order. Monck's control of civilian affairs was removed when a Council was set up in Scotland in September 1655. This regime lasted until the death of Oliver Cromwell in 1660 and, although it depended very much on the continual presence of Monck and his army, it enabled the country to be run in a stable manner in all spheres of activity which was more than it had enjoyed for many years.

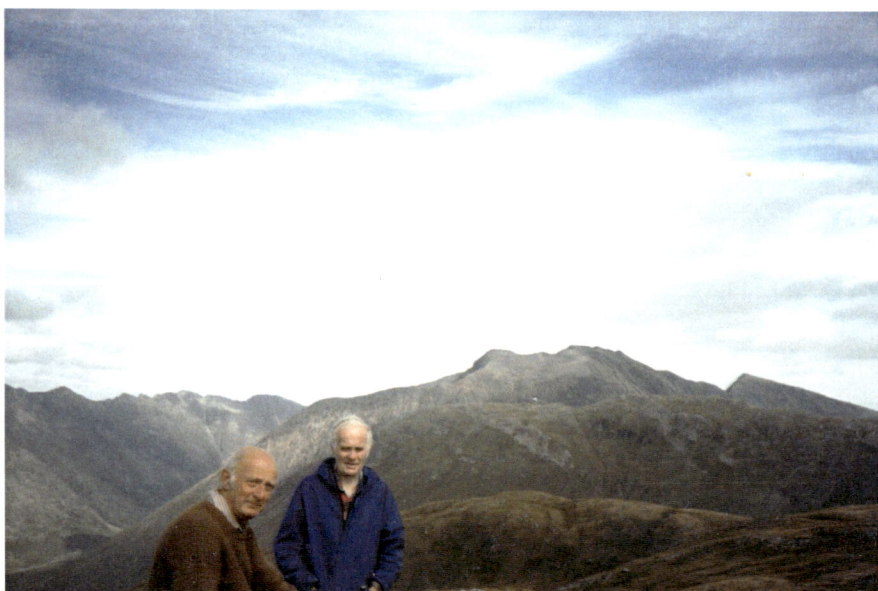

Meall Lighighe and the Hills of Glencoe

McGregors, McDonalds and Campbells

Glen Strae, Glen Orchy, Glen Lyon and Glencoe

In historical terms I feel that this area 'belongs' to the McGregors, of whom the most renowned is Rob Roy, pictured by Sir Walter Scott. Although Rob Roy's grave at Balquhidder is a great tourist attraction the Braes of Balquhidder are not the main McGregor country. The ancestral homelands of the clan are in the area around Glen Strae and Glen Orchy. J. Forbes McGregor,in his history of the McGregor clan, has researched the origins of the clan, whose motto is 'My Blood is Royal', in an attempt to determine their royal descent from the time of Kenneth Macalpin. In the course of his researches he records that for several hundred years the main clan country was in Glen Strae, where the chieftain had his home in the village of Stronmilchan. It was in the graveyard of the old Glen Orchy church that the chieftains of the Glen Strae line were all buried.

Glen Lyon and Glencoe

About the end of the thirteenth century the main Glen Strae line of McGregors came to an end with a chief's daughter who had married a Campbell. While the Campbells then held the legal title to the land, the McGregors held it by the power of the sword, certainly up to the end of the fifteenth century. But the McGregors were failing to keep pace with the changing political situation in Scotland and, eventually, the clan lost possession of all its lands and the Glen Strae lands passed to the Campbells.

In the course of time two substantial offshoots of the clan sprang up in the Roro area of Glen Lyon and in the Loch Rannoch area. As only the Glen Strae chiefs were buried in the old Glen Orchy church graveyard, each of these subsidiary clans had their own burial place for the sub-chiefs. The Rannoch group had their burial place at Killiechonan on the north side of Loch Rannoch and the Roro section were buried at Brenudh in Glen Lyon. So it was a natural progression to go from Glen Strae and Glen Orchy to Glen Lyon.

Glen Lyon

Glen Lyon (*Map 22*) itself has very happy memories for me, as my last pre-war hill-walking expedition included a crossing from Glen Lochay to Cashlie in Glen Lyon where we set up our small Black's 'One Guinea' tent ready to tackle Stuchd an Lochain the following day. It is strange to think that my grandchildren hardly know what a guinea means and that the tent really did cost a guinea. The same tent is still used by them on the back green to play with, over sixty years later. I can recall with awe the magnificent view we got from the summit the following day which dawned bright clear and cold as befits a good March day.

Glen Lyon has everything; strong connections with the history of Scotland, records of clan warfare, castles, churches and bells, standing stones, the legends of Fionn, and of course the attractive but unlikely story that Pontius Pilate was born in Fortingall when his Father was there on a visit to a Scottish chieftain. It has its sparkling river, its lochs, its narrow passes and the great Munros which dominate it on both sides and at its top. It also includes a group of the Corbetts. I cannot recall a walk which did not have its special enjoyable feature.

The book I like best about Glen Lyon is 'Highland Perthshire' by Duncan Fraser and I have based my exploration of the Glen on this book and have used much of its lore for my descriptions. There is so much to choose from that I found it difficult to decide what aspect to associate with the Corbetts.

In his book Duncan Fraser quotes an old Gaelic saying - 'Twelve castles had Fionn in the crooked glen of the stones'. This is what decided me to look for the various unique stones to be found in Glen Lyon.

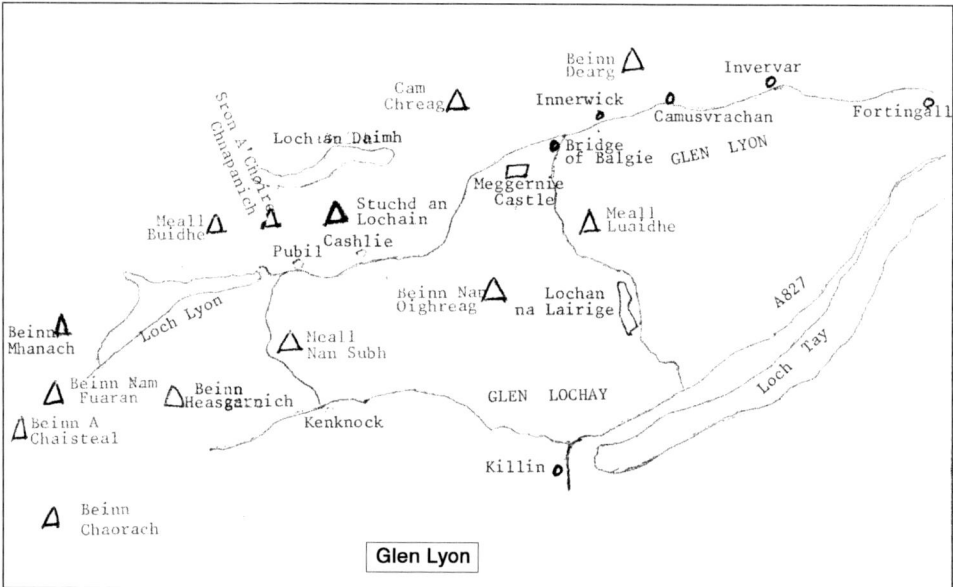

Map 22

The Bhacain Stone

Four of the famous Fionn castles are quite close to the road at Pubil and not far from them is the famous Bhacain stone. It is not a tall stone, probably under three feet high, but it is shaped like the head of a hound. Legend has it that this was the stone to which Fionn and his warriors tethered their hounds when returning to their fort after a hunt. Indeed one of the forts nearby is called Caisteal coin-a- Bhacain -the castle of the dogs' stake.

Duncan Fraser tells in his book, how even in relatively recent times this stone was considered to have mysterious powers. For instance, it was claimed that any girl creeping under its head achieved the same result as the modern day use of contraceptive pills – a reputation just as likely to be substantiated as the claims of Fortingall to be the birthplace of Pontius Pilate.

Meggernie Castle

On our way down the glen we passed close to Meggernie Castle whose history is so interesting. The item in Duncan Fraser's book which

104

took my fancy was the rather amazing coincidences surrounding the wife of the grandson of Mad Colin Campbell. This lady produced one Campbell son, Robert, before she was left a widow. She remarried a McGregor and amongst their family was a daughter who also married a McGregor and presented her mother with a McGregor grandson. Sadly the lady was widowed a second time but married a third time. By this third marriage she had a daughter who was married to the son of the MacDonald chief in Glencoe. The coincidence is that the son of the first marriage was none other than the notorious Captain Campbell who was in charge of the troops at the massacre of Glencoe and he and his step- sister had some very different parts to play in the massacre. The McGregor grandson, by the second marriage, had also his place in history as he was none other than the most famous of the McGregors, Rob Roy himself. This remarkable grandmother had also a famous stone associated with her at her funeral. On his mother's death the notorious Captain Campbell decided that she should have a funeral to be remembered. All the connections of her three marriages were invited to the ceremony in Glen Lyon. The interment was preceded by a full scale Highland Games. To his consternation Captain Campbell had to witness a McGregor putting the stone far beyond any of the Campbell or other competitors. However Captain Campbell had a trick up his sleeve and he proposed to continue the games the next day. Over night a huge Campbell shepherd living up the glen was summoned hurriedly and in the morning, to the Captain's delight he putted the stone far beyond his McGregor opponent. Such were the celebrations that the lady's interment had to be delayed yet another day. A fitting finale to a remarkable lady.

Beinn Dearg and Meall Luaidhe (Now renamed Meall nam Maigheach)

Proceeding down theGlen leads one to Bridge of Balgie whence I had planned to ascend three Corbetts; **Meall Luaidhe**- really an outlier of Ben Lawers, **Beinn nan Oighreag**, and on the north side of the glen **Beinn Dearg**. My enthusiastic Munro climbing friend from Bradford wanted to climb the four Carn Mairg Munros. Coming up from Bradford he picked me up at Edinburgh and we were ready at Invervar to start our respective walks at 10 a.m. Our calculations were such that with his greater walking speed he would be able to complete the Carn Mairg round by 4 p.m. and in that time I ought to be able to drive to the foot of Beinn Dearg and after climbing that hill drive up the Bridge of Balgie road and climb Meall Luaidhe. I would have to leave Beinn nan Oighreag for another day.

Leaving my friend to his Munros I drove to the small church at Innerwick from where a good right of way runs over to Loch Rannoch. The church at Innerwick is well worth a visit but on this occasion as a time schedule was involved I merely parked the car outside the church.

Glen Lyon and Glencoe

Beinn Dearg

The right of way goes up the Lairig Ghallabhaich and it had been my intention to strike off the Lairig east up a small tributary of the Allt Ghallabhaich . Near it however, I found an excellent forest track which took me comfortably up onto the plateau, near a cairn in the bealach between Creag Ard and Beinn Dearg. From here it was a gentle climb to the summit. But the visibility was poor and all I was rewarded with was a good view of the western slopes of Carn Gorm over whose top I hoped that Wilf had by now passed . Because of the poor visibility and because of my time schedule I abandoned my intention to descend by the ridge from Beinn Dearg leading to Camusvrachan where there was another of the famous Glen Lyon stones. This is the Bodach Chraig Fiannaidh – a heavy rounded stone with another flat stone beside it at a slightly higher level. It was a test of manhood for a youth to be able to lift the rounded stone up onto the flat stone. In his book, Duncan Fraser records that there are similar testing stones at Cashlie and at Lochs. I returned to the car by the convenient road by which I had ascended and proceeded to the Bridge of Balgie road.

Meall Luaidhe (Now renamed Meall nam Maigheach)

I proceeded up the road leading across to Loch Tay and stopped where the road swung sharply to the east and managed to park the car in an old road metal recess. From here it was a steady ascent along some fairly uneven heathery ground to the summit of Meall Luaidhe where to my disappointment, I was greeted with a heavy mist and, very shortly afterwards, with a torrential storm of sleet and rain. In no time I was completely soaked and, of course, there was no view to be had. So, without delay, I set off back to the car. I tried to get some shelter from a stone dyke which aligns the descent but the storm was too much for that. Although it eased off I had no option but to make a complete change of my clothes before setting off to my time rendezvous at Invervar.

The Massacre of Glencoe

After the failure of the Glencairn rising, the Jacobite campaign really collapsed although the ashes of the campaign still smouldered on. The Government wanted peaceful conditions in Scotland in order to release regiments for the war against France. An attempt was therefore made to negotiate with the Highland chiefs still attached to the Jacobite cause. To encourage them to switch their allegiance, a financial inducement was proposed and the Earl of Breadalbane was given the task of meeting the chiefs and explaining the proposals. A meeting was held at Achallader

Glen Lyon and Glencoe

Castle with some of the chiefs and Breadalbane succeeded in obtaining their agreement. William then signed an order requiring an oath of allegiance to him to be taken by a certain date – 1st January, 1692. MacIan, Chief of the Glencoe Mcdonalds left it too late by a few days - partly due to bad weather, and did not sign until after the due date. This was just the excuse that some of his enemies required to get their revenge on him and his clan. The massacre was arranged and ordered by Dalrymple, Breadalbane and Argyll but William himself signed the order. The massacre took place in February 1692. It was a blatant breach of the long-established code of hospitality in the Highlands. Even so, it fell short of wiping out the clan as about ninety percent of the clan escaped. Not only did it fail in its nefarious main purpose but it backfired, as it raised doubts in the minds of the other chiefs who had already signed under the Achallader agreement. Also as William had signed the order himself Jacobite sympathies were in no way extinguished and the events of the next fifty years demonstrated this.

Meall Lighiche

The escape routes for the members of the MacDonald clan after the massacre were probably mostly to the south despite the adverse weather conditions and one of the places of refuge would be Glen Creran. I have therefore associated the Corbett in this areas with the Massacre.(*Map 23*)

We drove to Glencoe to tackle **Meall Lighiche**. We parked the car at the Gleann-leac na-muidhe road-end where we ascertained that we would not be interfering with any stalking by walking on the hill. Although we could have taken the car up the private road to the house, we decided to walk as it was a lovely day. It was so warm and set so fair at the top of the road that we parked our rucksacks there and set off up a rough path along the bank of the Allt na Muidhe towards the top of the outlier, Creag Bhan. We decided to aim for the col between

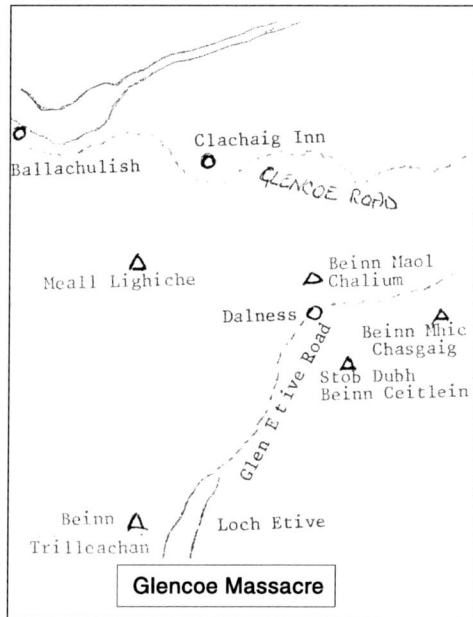

Map 23

this hill and Meall Lighiche but it was rather heavy going and we would have been better advised to keep to the ridge. However we had no difficulty in reaching the summit of the Corbett and also had no compunction in sitting down to admire the magnificent view of the superb Glencoe complex, the Mamores and Ben Nevis, and the Loch Creran Hills to the south.

We descended by the ridge and as we sat in the sun enjoying our mid-day snacks, we reflected on the grim snowbound conditions which the McDonalds, many of them clad in their night clothes, had experienced that dreadful morning. Close to where we were sitting the chief of the clan had his house where he was murdered. What hard times those were.

Tom on Beinn Each

The 1715 Jacobite Rising

This rising attracts much less attention that the more romantic 'Forty-five' and 'Bonnie Prince Charlie'. It was, in fact, a much stronger rising with both an English and a Scottish content and had it been more efficiently managed a Jacobite victory might well have been achieved. The rising was originally planned to consist of a south-west England rising under the Duke of Ormonde which was to have been the main effort. Diversionary risings were to take place in north-east England and in Scotland.

The English Risings
As a result of careless talk by the Jacobites, the Government were quickly able to deal with the main south-west England rising which soon collapsed. The north-east section of the English rising, however, went

ahead and James Vlll was proclaimed King at Warkworth. This force was unable to capture Newcastle and headed north by Rothbury, Eslington, Brandon and Wooler to Kelso. At Kelso they were joined by the redoubtable soldier Mackintosh of Borlum and his Highlanders who had been sent south to help the English by the Earl of Mar. Sadly they could not agree about the leadership of the force and the experienced 'Old Borlum' was ignored. From Kelso, they marched via Jedburgh, Hawick and Langholm, passing close to the slopes of the Donald, Cauldcleuch Head en route. Then they marched south avoiding Carlisle and succeeded in capturing Preston. But here they were surrounded by strong Government forces and compelled to surrender, bringing the English section of the Fifteen to an ignominious ending.

The Main Scottish Rising

This was created effectively by one man, the Earl of Mar, largely for his own potential benefit. He had been dismissed from his political posts and been snubbed by George I and he transferred his support to James VIII because he hoped to regain his positions through a Jacobite restoration. He was known as 'Bobbing Johnny' because of his ability to retain his political power under changes of government.

There can be no doubt that he was a man of great ability. After his snub from George I, he returned to Scotland and arranged a tinchal (or deer hunt) in Glen Buchat, overlooked by the Ladder range of hills with their Corbett, **Carn Mor** (*Map 24*). Several of the leading Jacobite chiefs did not accept his invitation to the tinchal as he did not hold a commission from James VIII. There is some suggestion that he then forged a preliminary commission and arranged another tinchal on his own land in Mar. The clan chiefs no doubt enjoyed some good deer hunting in this country and the punch brewed in 'The Devil's Punchbowl' in Glen Quoich is reputed to have been used to toast the health of James VIII. The attractive Corbett in Glen Quoich is **Carn na Drochaide** and in the Mar country there is also **Sgor Mor**.

The 'Tinchal' Corbetts
Carn Mor

As I travelled back to Edinburgh one afternoon, the glorious sunshine at the Lecht simply called out not to be wasted. The ski-path led up to the top of Meikle Corr Riabhach and from there a boundary fence went all the way to the summit of Carn Liath passing over the almost dry Coachan Crom. Round about here a cairn marks the end of the boundary fence (between Banff and Aberdeen) although a subsidiary fence goes off to the North-west. A gentle slope led to the top of Monadh an t'Sluichd Leith

The 'Fifteen'

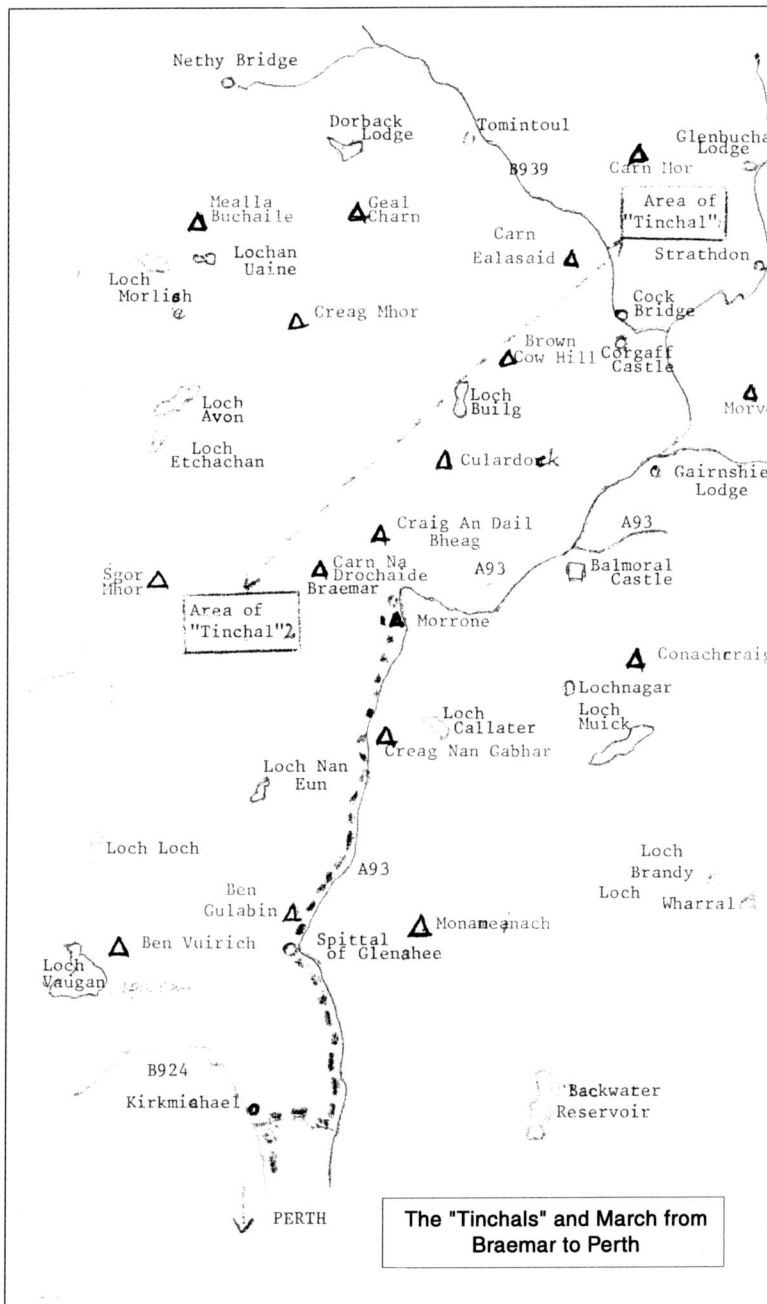

The "Tinchals" and March from Braemar to Perth

Map 24

111

whence it is only about a mile to the ordnance survey pillar at the top of Carn Mor.

I enjoyed clear views all round - the Ben Rinnes group to the north and the eastern Cairngorms to the west. The names of the little crofts in the valley below caught my fancy - Clash of Scalan on the slopes of Tom Trumper, Duffdefiance below Finlate Hill, and unusually named Relaquheim with Baronet's Cairn to the south. The Ladder Hill ridge provided delightful walking and all the way along I was accompanied by a melodious and plaintive chorus from the numerous golden plovers.

Carn na Drochaide

This hill is attractively situated to the north of Braemar and is conveniently accessible by car. Indeed I was optimistically planning a 'three Corbett' day if I could get my car close enough to Culardoch and Craig an Dail Bheag after climbing Carn na Drochaide. I started the day by driving round by the Linn of Dee to Allanaquoich where I parked my car and had a look at the Linn of Quoich and the famous Punch Bowl. I continued up the bank of the stream until I was clear of the trees. An up and down but pleasant walk over the slope of Carn Dearg led to the summit plateau of Carn na Drochaide, really cluttered with cairns. However there was little doubt about the summit cairn. It was a delightful day of sunshine and the walk down to the car gave extensive views of the valley.

Sgor Mor

For the other Mar Forest Corbett, I was accompanied at the outset by my friend Wilf, who was planning to walk over from Braemar to the Aviemore ski-slope car park climbing Derry Cairngorm, Ben Macdhui and Cairngorm on the way. We planned that he would use my folding cycle to cycle up to Derry Lodge from the Linn of Dee and leave the cycle at the bridge over the River Luibeg for me to pick up after I had climbed Sgor Mor. We estimated that in the time he would take to reach the ski-slope car park, I would be able to climb Sgor Mor, pick up the cycle, cycle back to the car at Linn of Dee, and then drive over to the ski-slope car park to meet him. We had successfully tried several of these joint enterprises previously but the timing for this one was a little uncertain.

Wilf set off on the cycle from the Linn of Dee car park and I followed on foot. In a short distance I cut off the Derry Lodge road through the pine woods to Carn an' lc Duibhe. From here it was splendid walking in sunshine over the plateau to Sgor Mor. It was very thirsty weather and I had filled my flask before I left in anticipation of this, enabling me to enjoy a leisurely and comfortable stop on the summit. On the way down, I kept on the ridge in the sun over to Sgor Dubh even though I realised that it would lead me to a very steep slope down to the Luibeg bridge. Steep indeed it was but not difficult in the dry conditions and I duly found the cycle at the bridge. I enjoyed the largely freewheel cycle down the glen to the car at the Linn of Dee and a non-stop drive from there to the Cairngorm ski-slope car park got me there almost coinciding with Wilf's arrival – a very satisfying piece of hill-walking logistics.

The Royal Standard at Braemar

There was more support for Mar by now and he raised the Royal Standard in Braemar in September 1715, on the slopes of the Corbett, **Morrone**. *(Map 24)* Some days later, on the way to Perth, James VIII was proclaimed King at Kirkmichael. En route Corbett **Creag nan Gabhar** would be passed on the left and nearing Kirkmichael, Corbett **Ben Gulabin** would be traversed.

There was a much broader support for the Fifteen compared to the later Forty-five and a considerable number of Lowland leaders supported Mar. Sadly, the Earl of Mar lacked military knowhow and was really a politician and not a battle commander. Although he captured Perth, Mar showed no great sense of urgency and remained too long there largely occupied in organisational matters. He succeeded, however, in raising a strong force for the Jacobites and had he been Chief of Staff to an inspirational Army Commander, as De Guingand was to Montgomery in World War II, then the Fifteen could have followed a very different course.

Morrone

Although there is good access to this Corbett from Braemar, we were combining it with Corbett Creag nan Gabhar in Glen Clunie. We parked the car near Coldrach and took the stalker's path leading up the east side of Morrone. There was a considerable depth of snow but a tracked vehicle had been up the path before us and had compacted the soft snow and thus made the walking much easier. The summit ridge was soon reached and shortly after re-orienting ourselves to progress along it, we were surprised to pick up a road leading right to the summit. The summit is cluttered up with a meteorological station, a television relay pylon, two huts and a plaque defining the extent of the National reserve along with a summit cairn.

Creag nan Gabhar

This Corbett with Morrone, provided one of the rare 'multiple Corbett' days. We parked the car near Glen Clunie Lodge and walked up the little Alltamhait valley at the head of which we took a series of bearings circling us round to the summit of Creag nan Gabhar. Had it been clear we had hoped for views of Loch Callater where I had camped over fifty years ago. Looking at the walk I then undertook, carrying a substantial rucksack over Carn an Turc, Cairn of Claise, Tom Buidhe and Tolmount into Glen Doll and down Glen Clova brought home to me my deterioration with age.

Ben Gulabin

The next Corbett on the route to Kirkmichael is Ben Gulabin. To climb it, I drove from Edinburgh to the Spittal of Glenshee. I parked at the roadside at a point marked 1255 on my map, where a stream coming down from the north side of Ben Gulabin flows into the Allt a Ghlinnie Bhig. The stream came down a ravine with very steep banks and we followed the top of the south bank up to the bealach between Ben Gulabin and Creagan Bheithe. A straightforward ascent in mist over a considerable snowfield took us uneventfully to the summit. The cairn itself was surrounded by a sheltering wall but gave us no protection as it was full of snow.

The Rising in the West of Scotland

In the West of Scotland, MacDonald of Glengarry called out his clan, as he had promised Mar at one of the tinchals and Mar, as he had in turn promised, sent General Gordon, a soldier with considerable European experience to marshal as many of the clans as possible. Only the Grants from Glen Moriston initially joined Glengarry. The route followed by the MacDonalds is not firmly established. However as they were linking up with the Grants they would likely cut across the hills from Glen Garry to join them at the head of Loch Lochy, passing over the slopes of **Ben Tee**. They then appear to have marched down the Great Glen to make an abortive attack on Inverlochy garrison. The clansmen were forced to withdraw and, as is described later, may well have continued their march through the Lairig Leacach, passing **Cruach Innse** and **Sgurr Innse**, from Spean Bridge over to the head of Loch Treig.

Here they were joined by the McGregors, the MacDonalds of Clanranald, the Camerons and the Stewarts of Appin. General Gordon had now a considerable force under his control and decided to make an attempt to capture Inverary but neither attackers nor defenders displayed much military skill and the attack was called off. Gordon then marched his force over to Auchterarder to join up with Mar. Once again their route is not established but probably by Glen Fyne and Glen Falloch, passing Corbett Meall an Fhudair.

The 'Fifteen'

General Gordon's clansmen probably crossed the River Falloch at Invernarnan and followed up the Ben Glas Burn into the head waters of the Lochlarig River. This stream flows to the north of Corbett **Stob a' Choin** until it enters the west end of Loch Doine. The clansmen continued by Loch Voil near Corbett **Stob Fear-Tomhais** to Strathyre. Then possibly they marched through Glen Artney to Muthill and Auchterarder passing close to the slopes of Corbetts **Ben Each and Meall na Fearna**. At Auchterarder they joined up with Mar. On the whole the rising in the west of Scotland was pretty ineffectual.

Ben Tee
Murray and I set out from Edinburgh one morning to climb Ben Tee among other hills in the area. We drove up the small road to Kilfinnan Farm, followed the north bank of the Kilfinnan Burn being careful to keep out of the waterfall gully, and continued almost due north until we reached Lochan Diota. This was our selected point for turning west up the slopes of Ben Tee itself. The going was very rough and as we reached the summit the mist came down and we did not stay long. This was a disappointment as we had looked forward to a splendid Corbett viewpoint.

If there was to be a contest for the most shapely Munro, Corbett, Donald or unclassified hill, then I would be including Ben Tee as one of my nominations. I do not know how it would fare among other likely contestants such as Schiehallion or Ben A'an or Ben Stack, to mention some of my other favourites, but there can be little doubt that Ben Tee has its own special shapeliness.

Sgurr Innse and Cruach Innse
To climb the Corbetts, Cruach Innse and Sgurr Innse, we started from Spean Bridge and crossed the river, driving on to Corriecollie farm. We passed through the farm and drove up over the old railway until we came to some locked forestry gates where we parked the car. An attractive path then took us through the fine pine and larch woods until we reached a bealach at about 1650 feet. Here we turned north east to the bealach between the two Corbetts and climbed Sgurr Innse first. There was a fairly steep path but it was clearly marked and we came down the same way to proceed to Cruach Innse. It was an easy scramble up and down Cruach Innse and in the fine sunshine we enjoyed good views of the Grey Corries and the Loch Treig Munros.

Stob a'Choin
At Inverarnan Terry and I took the car up to the small car-park at Inverlochlarig Farm and walked up to Blaircreich Farm where we crossed

the Allt Sgionie and followed a pronounced ridge to Bealach Coire an Laoigh due east of the summit. The slopes of Stob a' Choin are somewhat craggy and there were a few icy snow patches which required care. Terry did not have satisfactory climbing boots and had some difficulty on these icy bits and also with the steep and interesting little scramble which took us to the top of Stob a'Choin in rather dull conditions.

Stob Fear- Tomhais
(Previously wrongly named Ceann Na Baintighearna)
On my Ordnance Map (revised 1933) Ceann na Baintighearna is the name of a top shown as 2277 feet high but there is clearly a higher point, shown at 2526 feet, unnamed on my map, about a mile to the south. This discrepancy has been observed by the Scottish Mountaineering Club in their latest revision of the Corbett list and the hill has been named as above. It is locally known as the 'surveyor's peak' and the Gaelic translation of this has been adopted as the name for the hill.

This peak, like others in the Strathyre area, makes a very pleasant outing from Edinburgh. I tempted my English friend Terry to have another hillwalk. From Strathyre we drove along the slow moving River Balvaig and turned up an attractive little glen, Glen Buckie, parking the car at Ballimore Farm at the top of the glen. Here we crossed the Calair Burn and followed a south westerly bearing until we came to the Allt Gleann Dubh. After crossing this stream by a bridge not marked on my old map, a pleasant up and down ridge takes one to the summit. This little known hill provided a magnificent Corbett viewpoint, particularly of the Trossachs area hills and my particular favourites Ben Vorlich and Stuc a'Chroin. The Crianlarich group was dominated by Ben More and Stob Binnein but apart from Munros we enjoyed the views of Stob a' Choin and Meall an t'Seallaidh.

Beinn Each and Meall na Fearna
Although it involves a fairly steep climb from the Ardchullarie More track to Glen Ample to get onto the slopes of Beinn Each, Meall na Fearna and later Beinn Bhreac, this is probably the most direct route from Strathyre to Auchterarder via Glen Artney. At the time of the Fifteen rebellion it is difficult to say how the state of afforestation then would compare with to-day. However, this was a likely route for the clansmen under General Gordon as it leads into the head waters of the Keltie Water, round to Arivurichardich.

This superbly sounding name brings back a long series of happy memories. When I first climbed Ben Vorlich and Stuc a'Chroin, the route we chose was by Arivurichardich cottage then occupied by a shepherd and his young family. On one occasion I recall a Highland packman carrying his wares on his horse displaying them to the good-wife.

Beinn Each

From Loch Lubnaig, Murray, celebrating his first great – grandfatherhood, and I, accompanied by his son Alan , took the path towards Beinn Each. I had always wondered why Beinn Each, shown on my 1927 map to have a height of 2660 feet, was not a Corbett but I presumed that it was being treated as an outlier of Stuc a'Chroin. However the Scottish Mountaineering Club have recently promoted it to be a Corbett in its own right. We could see a lot of heavy snow on the slopes of Stuc a'Chroin but without difficulty reached the bealach above Coire nan Saighead and on to the summit of Beinn Each. We got the great views of Ben Ledi and the other peaks that we had expected.

Meall na Fearna

With my daughter Anne, her husband Ken and one of their daughters, Alison, we drove to Ardvorlich on the south side of Loch Earn and took the now well-worn path leading up to Ben Vorlich. At the fork in the path we carried on up the pass with Ben Vorlich on our right. At the top of the pass we continued a bit further towards Dubh Chorein so that we could strike north east up a small stream and hopefully avoid some of the rough ground. We were reasonably successful in our efforts and it wasn't long before we had reached the Meall na Fearna summit.

The Closing Stages of the 'Fifteen'

From Perth, Mar dispatched Mackintosh of Borlum to help the English Jacobites in Northumberland as already mentioned. Mackintosh's crossing of the Forth to march on to Kelso was a great military success and much enhanced Mar's prestige at the time.

So far as the main Scottish campaign was concerned Mar was, despite his substantial forces, very slow to march south from Perth. When he eventually marched to Stirling he was surprised to find that the Government forces were already in position at Sheriffmuir, at the west end of **the Ochil Donalds**. (*Map 25)* The ensuing battle was somewhat of a shambles and neither general could take any credit for generalship. Both sides could claim victory.

Nonetheless, Mar was stopped from going any further south and this was really the end of the Fifteen rising. Although James VIII later landed in North Scotland he was a very uninspiring leader and in a few weeks he returned to the continent. Mar then retreated to the north from Perth and the clans gradually returned to their homes from Inverness. The Fifteen rising was over.

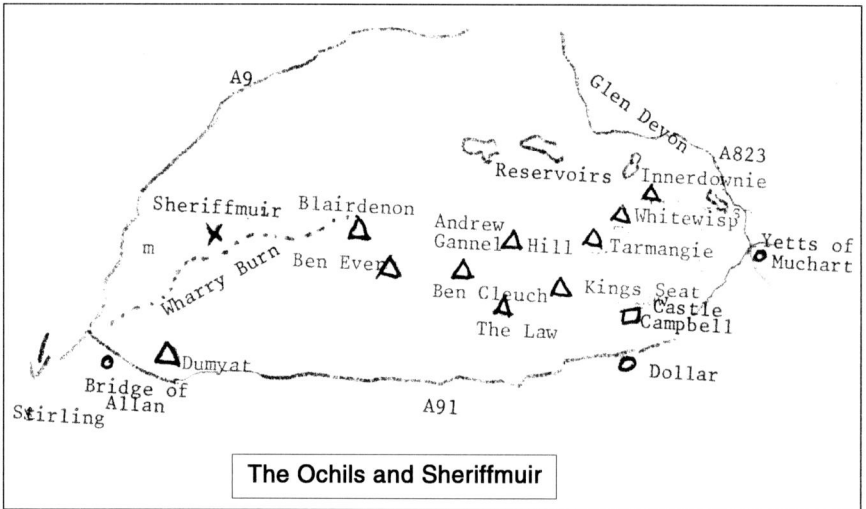

Map 25

The Ochil Donalds

We decided to do a traverse of the Ochil Donalds in one day by using two cars. In thick mist we optimistically left one car at the bridge over the Wharry Burn on the battlefield of Sheriffmuir with all its memories of the Fifteen. In the other car, we drove round to Glen Devon and parked at the side of the Castlehill Reservoir.

Our optimism proved to be justified as the mist began to lift as we walked up to the Glen Quey reservoir. We climbed up, via Glen Foret Hill, to Innerdownie and happily the mist cleared away. Pleasant walking took us along via Bentie Knowe to Whitewisp Hill. The next top, Tarmangie was reached without dropping below 2000 feet. From there, we dropped down to the Muddy Moss, an appropriately named place where three burns meet to form the Burn of Sorrow. Then came King's Seat with its substantial cairn . At the bealach below we ate our sandwiches before climbing Andrew Gannel Hill. It was still so beautifully sunny at the top of Andrew Gannel Hill that we decided to stick to the ridge instead of going direct to The Law. At The Law, mist began to gather in the valley below but we remained above it for a time.

The 'Fifteen'

However it climbed more quickly than we did and when we reached the summit of Ben Cleuch we found ourselves in thick mist for the first since we had left the car at the Wharry Burn. We had to make use of our compasses to find the route to Ben Ever. There was a substantial drop to the Glenwinmill Burn followed by periods of pretty rough ground over to the plateau leading up to Blairdenon Hill. The last stretch took us down from Blairdenon Hill over Mickle Corin to the Wallace Stone and thence to the Wharry Burn and the car.

The Ochils – so called after the Celtic word Uchel, meaning high ground – provide a set of views peculiar to themselves, over the Lomonds and the Cleish Hills and over the Forth to the Pentland range. It is said to be possible to see both Ben Nevis and the Cairngorms from the tops but I have never been so fortunate.

Conachcraig and slopes of Lochnagar

The 1745 Rising

'The Forty-Five'

James VIII, as he grew older, became an even less inspiring leader of the Jacobite cause than he was in the Fifteen. But in 1719, he had married Clementina Walkinshaw, a Polish King's granddaughter and two sons resulted from the marriage; 'Bonnie Prince Charlie' and his younger brother Prince Henry. Prince Charles was an energetic, good looking and fit young man.

In 1740 the European political situation favoured the Jacobite cause and the King of France once again thought of sending armed forces to invade England to try to force the withdrawal of the British armies fighting on the continent in the War of the Austrian succession. Prince Charles made an ideal 'figurehead' leader for such a diversionary attack which was scheduled to be under the command of Marshal Saxe, one of the outstanding military commanders of his time. Bad weather and the power of the British navy forced the abandonment of this plan.

The 1745 Rising

The Start of the Expedition

However Prince Charles was not to be denied and formed an expedition of his own to land in Scotland. He hoped that the support he expected to receive from the Scottish Jacobites would persuade the French to mount a contemporaneous attack in England. With two ships and a small band of supporters, Prince Charles set off for Scotland. Once again the British Navy intervened and a British warship engaged the French warship accompanying Prince Charles. Both warships were so badly damaged in their engagement that they had to return to port for repairs. Prince Charles determinedly continued his voyage on the other ship. He landed on the small island of Eriskay and here the local Jacobite chiefs tried to persuade him to abandon his attempt. But whatever may have been his other failings, Prince Charles had courage and determination, qualities which his Father and his Grandfather had both lacked. He refused to withdraw and sailed on across to the mainland where he landed on the shore of Loch nan Uamh. Here again the clan chiefs tried to dissuade him but he continued to refuse and gradually he began to receive promises of support - largely from the McDonalds in the early stages.

The Glenfinnan Rendezvous

Despite the rather unencouraging support, the Prince fixed on Glenfinnan *(Map 26)* as a rendezvous for the clan chiefs. From Borradale on the shore of Loch nan Uamh, Prince Charles moved down to Kinlochmoidart where some of his supporters were gathering. From Kinlochmoidart, Prince Charles marched to the shore of Loch Shiel and was then transported up the narrow Loch in a small rowing boat. The very smallness of the boat must have magnified the impression of the superb surrounding Corbetts there. He landed at his rendezvous in Glenfinnan, where the Royal Standard was raised.

Glenfinnan and Kinlochmoidart
The Eastern Lochshiel Corbetts and the Kinlochmoidart trio

I had already been forced to abandon the two eastern Loch Shiel Corbetts, **Sgurr Craobh a'Chaorainn and Sgurr Ghuibhsachain**, as I had been blocked in by an unexpected snow storm at Glen Hurich where I was staying in the Resourie Bothy. I was anxious to make another attempt and I therefore planned a round trip beginning at Glenfinnan and circling round to Moidart. I intended to make Glenfinnan the base for the Loch Shiel Corbetts and Glen Uig for the Kinlochmoidart trio, **Rois-Bhein, Sgurr na Ba Glaise and An Stac.**

Streap △   △ Braigh   Meall A
Sgurr Na Utha   Nan   Phubuill
                     Uamhachan
                  △
Loch Nan
Uamh   Glenfinnan
Sound
of   An Stac   Loch Eilt
Arisaig   △ Beinn Mhic
              Cedidh   Fassfern
        Glen Uig Rois △ Sgurr Na △ Beinn Odhar
              Bheinn Ba Glaise △ Bheag   Loch Eil
Loch Moidart   Kinlochmoidart   Sgorr Craobh
                        Loch Shiel   △ A Chaoruinn
                                  Sgurr Ghuibhsachain

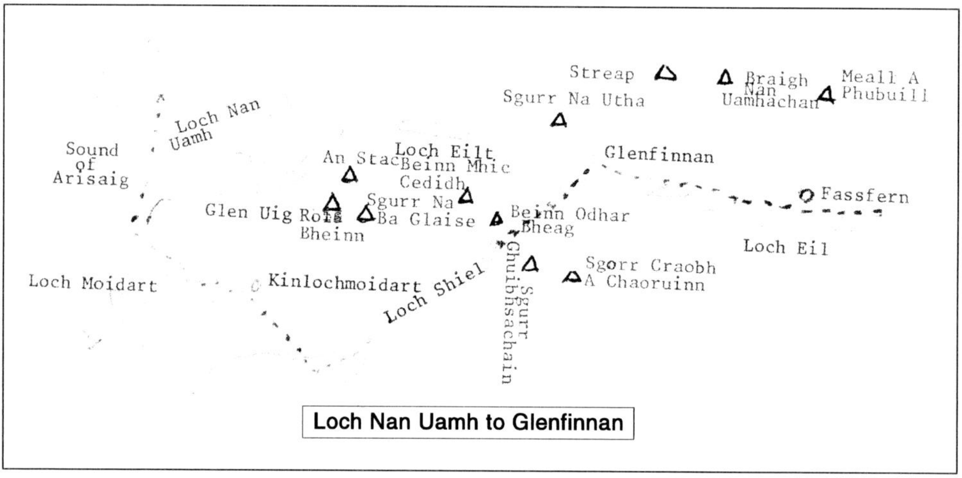

Loch Nan Uamh to Glenfinnan

Map 26

Sgorr Craobh a' Chaorainn and Sgurr Ghuibhsachain

I took my car along to the Callop road end and my dog, Francie, and I set off along a good track by the west side of the Allt na Cruachie. Mist and rain began to descend as we branched off up the crags of Meall na Cuartaige and the summit of Sgurr Craobh a'Chaorainn was in thick mist when we reached it. The descent to the bealach and the ascent to the top of Sgurr Ghuibhsachain seemed relatively straightforward. At the bealach, however, Francie suddenly raised some deer and shot off into the mist after them. No amount of shouting and whistling could bring her back. The summit was not far away but I was anxious about Francie and worried that she might chase some of the sheep, which were down in the keeper's paddock. I reluctantly retraced my steps and went in to ask the keeper if he had noticed his sheep being roused by Francie on her return if indeed she had come that way. He had, however, noticed nothing and was not at all concerned about the dog who, he assured me, would easily find her way back on her own.

I was invited in to the house, where Mrs. Macrae produced a welcome cup of tea. After thanking Mrs. Macrae, I cycled back to the car where, much to my relief and delight, Francie awaited me. So I had to cycle back to Mr. Macrae and tell him that he had been quite right about the dog's capabilities.

The 1745 Rising

I was annoyed at having been so near and yet failing to reach the summit of Sgurr Ghuibhsachain so I planned an immediate second attempt. As a change I chose a route starting from Loch Sheil side. The following morning brought a complete change of conditions and it was in fine sunshine that I cycled down the good forestry road along Loch Sheil to Guesachan where I left my cycle. With Francie I proceeded up the slopes of Meall a Choire Chruinn, followed by an excellent ridge walk, where I was able to have a little scrambling in splendid sunshine. The views over Loch Sheil and its western Corbetts the Rois- Bheinn trio and the Ardgour summits enabled me to get a good idea of the summits still ahead of me. When one gets weather like this, there is no rush to get off the summit and this was no exception.

It was a beautiful evening when, after dinner at the comfortable little Inn at Glen Uig, I strolled along the shore of the loch looking out over the Sound of Arisaig with Eigg, Muck, and Rhum clear in the evening sun. A calm and settled evening was hopefully a good augury for the eagerly anticipated trio the next day.

Rois- Bheinn, Sgurr na Ba Glaise and An Stac

How quickly weather changes in this part of the world. I woke up to hear heavy rain hammering on the bedroom roof and after a leisurely breakfast reluctantly set off still in heavy rain, hoping against hope that the forecast of continued rain might not be accurate. I had decided to climb up the side of the Alisary burn and swing south up Coire na Criamh to the double bealach, one below An Stac and the other, Bealach an Fiona, between Sgurr na Ba Glaise and Rois- Bheinn. I found a rough track up the south side of the stream and followed this up to an imposing waterfall. A dry stone dyke then eventually led to the Bealach na Fiona. At this stage the rain was even heavier, and the mist was so thick that I couldn't see the dog at the end of the extended lead I was using because of the presence of sheep. I decided that the meteorologists were likely correct and abandoned Rois- Bheinn and confined my effort to Sgurr na Ba Glaise and An Stac. With careful compass work, I found the broad ridge to Sgurr na Ba Glaise and was relieved to be able to find its summit cairn in the atrocious conditions. After a quick snack in the dubious shelter of the cairn, I set off down to the lower bealach to tackle An Stac.

By now the rain had turned to sleet and I was soaked through. I duly found the lower bealach and thought that, as I was as wet as one could be, I might as well press on up An Stac, and set off in a northerly direction. I quickly had to abandon the attempt for an unusual reason. My climbing breeches had become so sodden with rain and sleet that my braces would no longer keep them up! Holding onto them as best I could I retraced my steps to the bealach and then squelched down to the car. An Stac and Rois-Bheinn had to remain on my list.

The Western Loch Shiel Corbetts and the Kinlochmoidart trio Beinn Mhic Cedidh, Beinn Odhar Bheag, Rois-Bheinn and An Stac

With the Rois-Bheinn and An Stac failure still on my mind I considered another attempt. I had been much attracted by the description in their book 'The Big Walks' by Ken Wilson and Richard Gilbert, of the walk over these tops from Glenfinnan to Glen Uig. After studying the times I would need, I decided to attempt the Beinn Mhic Cedidh, Beinn Odhar Bheag and Beinn Odhar Mhor group from Glenfinnan, returning to Glenfinnan, and once again climbing the Rois-Bheinn group from Glen Uig separately.

With this plan in mind we set off from Glenfinnan and left the car in a small car park just before the railway tunnels at Creag Gobhar. In brilliant sunshine, we walked along the railway track with my dog Francie. I did not, however, risk walking through the tunnels with her and, although this involved a bit of rough walking, it proved a wise precaution as an unexpected goods train came along. We heard it coming and secured the dog, receiving a wave and friendly toot from the driver as he passed. This is a very scenic stretch of railway where the beautiful views of Loch Eilt glittering in the sun are matched on the other side by the wild hillsides. Leaving the railway at the bridge over the Allt a Choin Bhuidhe, we continued up the west bank of the stream onto the steep north ridge of Beinn Mhic Cedidh. So far I had not been lucky with weather in Ardgour and Moidart but to-day the sun was shining at the summit. The Rois-Bheinn group was standing out splendidly and I could see what a superb cross-country walk it would have been. The ascent to the two Bein Odhars was obvious enough. A steepish descent to Bealach a Coire Rhuidhe followed by a similar climb to the top of Beinn Odhar Bheag presented no special difficulty and the summit of Beinn Odhar Bheag was attained to reveal the glories of Loch Sheil and its guardian hills.

It was a satisfying feeling to look over at my old friend Sgurr Ghuibhsachin dominating the east shore of the loch. All the Ardgour hills were clear and Ben Nevis in its grandeur was showing its snow covered top. The ridge along to Beinn Odhar Mhor looked very rough but it proved relatively easy and time and distance passed unnoticed with the distraction of scenery such as the Knoydart hills to the north. Indeed when it came to

The 1745 Rising

making our descent from Beinn Odhar Mhor to the car park, we were able to use Sgurr na Ciche as our guiding point. Altogether this was a very enjoyable walk and I began to think that I might well have managed 'The Big Walk'.

Once more I took the lovely run round by Loch Ailort to Glen Uig as the base for another attempt on RoisBheinn and An Stac. Once again the prospects seemed good as we strolled along the shores of the Sound of Arisaig in the fine evening sunshine. Once again, however, the weather changed rapidly and the morning dawned with low mist and rain. As a change from the Alisary burn approach, Hugh and I decided to use the west ridge of Rois- Bheinn starting from Roshven Farm. A steady ascent up into the mist took us to the west summit of the hill and we followed a dry stone dyke along to the east and main summit. By this time the weather had deteriorated further; the rain was much heavier and was now accompanied by a raging wind and the mist was very thick; the temperature had fallen and I could hardly hold the compass in my hand by the time we reached the summit of Rois- Bheinn. The gale intensified as we proceeded and with reluctance An Stac was abandoned for a second time.

It was two years before I could arrange a third trip and a fine spell of weather one July attracted me to the lovely run round Glenfinnan, Moidart and Sunart with the objective of An Stac, Ben Resipol and Garbh Bheinn. Third time was lucky and Sandy and I brushed through the fly infested ferns of the Alisary burn to reach the subsidiary bealach below Bealach na Fiona. From here we climbed direct to the summit of An Stac with some minor scrambling. Glorious views greeted us at the summit and we basked in the warmth. The Glenfinnan hills, the Moidart and Ardgour hills, the islands - Skye, Rhum, Eigg and Muck – Ben Nevis, of course, and a feast of other hills all round were enjoyed to the full. The sunshine was so warm and the air so balmy that we lazily didn't attempt the other two tops and just ambled back to the car where we had left two bottles cooling in the stream for our lunch.

The Arrival of the Clans

On arrival at Glenfinnan there were only about 200 supporters present when the Marquis of Tullibardine raised the Royal Standard. There has been some speculation as to the exact spot where the standard was raised but I don't feel that this is too important as one can stand at the monument and relive the disappointment that the young Prince must have felt when he had the support of only the Clanranald men . One can also imagine the thrill he must have experienced when he heard the pipes of the Cameron men as they marched down Glen Finnan. Lochiel had brought them over the pass beside that fine Corbett, **Streap**, and its nearby fellow, **Braigh nan Uamhachan**. *(Map 26)* The later arrival of more McDonalds and others must then have greatly boosted the Prince's morale.

Braigh nan Uamhachan and Streap

Some years previously I had walked up the Gleann Fionnlighe to climb Gulvain and I knew that the track was suitable for a cycle as far as Wauchan. I therefore used my cycle to help me up the glen and parked it a little beyond the bridge at Wauchan. The Na h' Uamhachan ridge is pleasant to walk on and is about two miles long. A short descent to a bealach leads to a mile long walk along the pronounced ridge of Sron Liath, leading directly to the summit of Braigh nan Uamhachan. There is a substantial stone wall along the ridge, at times shoulder high, reminiscent of the similar and remarkable one along the Garbh Chioch Mhor ridge in Glen Dessary. It was a delightful evening at the summit and had my leg not been troubling me I would have returned along the magnificent ridge, comprised of Streap Comhlaidh and Streap itself, to Stob Coire nan Cearc, fording the Dubh Lighe and contouring round the end of the Nam Uamhachan ridge to pick up my cycle. So I just enjoyed the views – Gulvain, the Glen Dessary hills and the rugged Knoydart group in the distance.

The 'score' to date for the Glenfinnan Corbetts was two in mist and rain with one dry. So Sandy and I were hoping that the law of averages would come into play and give us a good day for the magnificent Streap ridge. The law lived up to our expectations and it was a fine sunny day when we cycled up from Glenfinnan to Corryhully bothy where we parked our cycles. We could hardly believe our luck with the weather and it was obviously set so fine that we took the risk of leaving our rucksacks and spare clothes with the cycles. We walked up the path from the bothy until we spotted a small bridge over the River Finnan.

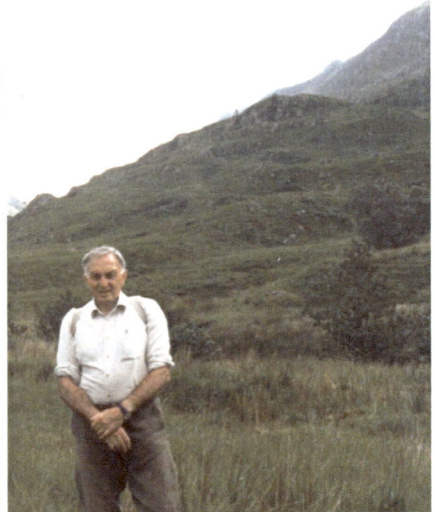

Sandy below the slopes of Streap

The 1745 Rising

_____

After crossing it we were forced to follow deer fencing round some new forestry, taking us off the bearing we wanted to follow. At the corner of the plantation we were able to get onto the bearing we needed and we contoured along rough ground until we struck the 'flake' referred to in the specialist guide books. This is just below Stob Coire nan Cearc and provides a good and not too steep ascent to the main ridge just a little way south-west of the summit. Unfortunately we were tempted to go straight to the summit ridge which looked quite close. This was a mistake as the route we took turned out to be very steep, and as usual, the ridge wasn't nearly so close as it looked. We decided to return down the 'flake' and at the end of it we angled steeply down to the Corryhully path. This was a particularly steep descent and I doubt if we would have taken that route in mist. We then thoroughly relished the lovely run down the glen on our cycles, comfortably freewheeling most of the way.

The March to Perth and Edinburgh

Almost immediately after the arrival of the Camerons and the MacDonalds, the army started to march along the shores of Loch Eil towards Loch Lochy (*Map 27*). The march took them past Fassfern where the Prince spent a night. This was the starting point that I used for the climb of Corbett **Meall a'Phubuill** up Gleann Suileag. The march, however, continued by Moy and Letterfinlay to Invergarry. Here there was a choice of going north to Inverness or south to the Atholl country and Edinburgh. News then arrived that General Cope was preparing to march through the   Corrieyairack Pass. This crystallised the discussion and a detachment was at once sent to secure the west end of the pass.

The Corrieyairack Pass has featured in many momentous episodes in Scottish history. There is some record of a battle fought by William the Lion at Garvamore; Montrose led his troops across the road up the pass before turning off to defeat the Argyll forces at Inverlochy; Bonnie Dundee, 'the first Jacobite', marched his Highland supporters through the pass. I have chosen to link the Pass with the Forty-five. Prince Charles led his troops across while Cope was on his way north to Inverness.

Cope had decided to march to Fort Augustus through the Corrieyairack but before he started he heard that the Jacobites had blocked the pass at its summit. Rightly, Cope abandoned any attempt to force his way through to Fort Augustus up the zig-zag pass, with Jacobites holding the summit. He therefore decided to go round by Inverness and down the Great Glen. The Jacobites didn't wait for him and, seeing the way open, they crossed the pass with its trio of Corbetts, **Corrieyairack, Gairbeinn** and **Meall na h'Aisre**. From Badenoch they continued down to Perth. Here the Prince was

127

joined by the able and active Lord George Murray who had considerable
military talents. He had fought in the Fifteen and the Nineteen and also
had several years experience of continental war. Sadly Prince Charles and
Lord George were unable to get on with one another. This undoubtedly
had a major effect on the conduct of the campaign. Had Lord George's
military skill been recognised by the Prince and his advice accepted the
Forty-five might well have succeeded.

From Perth the Jacobites continued to Edinburgh where the city was
captured but not the Castle. This success was followed up by the
overwhelming victory over the Government troops at Prestonpans. With
these successes Charles' army continued to increase in size although few
of the major nobles had yet committed themselves.

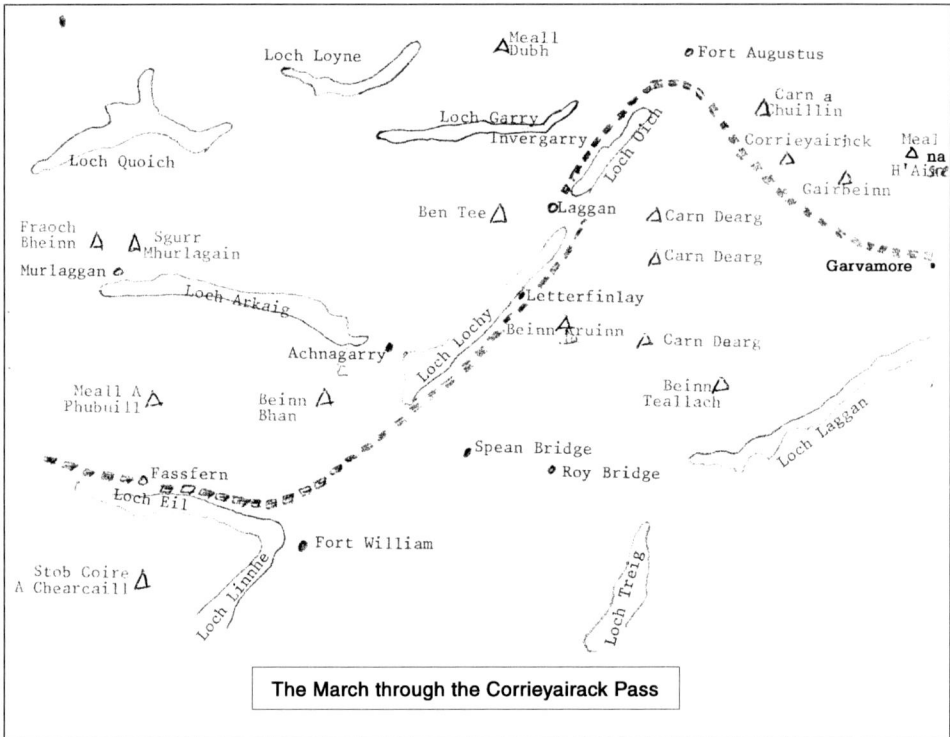

The March through the Corrieyairack Pass

Map 27

The 1745 Rising

_____

Meall a'Phubuill

I parked the car at Fassfern on Loch Eil and hoped that my folding cycle would be useable on the track marked on my old map leading up to Gleann Suileag. It turned out to be a good forestry track and I took my cycle as far as the turning point at the end of the forestry road. A rough track then followed to the bothy at Glensulaig. I went up to the bothy to inspect it's condition. I then returned to the bridge over the Suileag burn and followed a stalker's trackup the west side of the Allt Fionn Doire. The stream was running uncomfortably full so I was pleased to find a small bridge enabling me to cross without wading. This put me on the final slope to the summit which was reached in a raging gale, thick mist and really heavy rain. No view was to be had so I returned quickly to my cycle and pedalled back to the car uncomfortably wet.

The Corrieyairack Pass
Corrieyairack Hill, Gairbeinn and Meall na h'Aisre

The two western Corbetts of the Pass were approached from the Laggan Bridge end by driving the car up the old Wade road past Garvamore Bridge, to the end of the tarmacadam road at Melgarve. From here Hugh and I enjoyed the walk up the wild pass to its 2500 foot summit. As we ascended the zig-zags, we realised that Cope would have suffered a major defeat if he had tried to force his way through to Fort Augustus in the face of the Highlanders holding the heights above him. An old boundary fence leads easily to the summit of Corrieyairack Hill itself but the extensive westerly views that we had hoped for were sadly obscured by low cloud.

Luckily the clouds lifted enough for us to see the ridge ahead although there is no route finding difficulty and a short climb took us up to Geal Charn from where we followed the ridge and fence all the way to Gairbeinn. We then struck south and then south east to come out of the mist and descend comfortably to the car at Melgarve, over some rather boggy terrain.

We returned to Garvamore Bridge another day to climb Meall na h'Aisre and had the good luck to have a glorious day of sunshine. The ascent is quite uneventful up the side of the stream to the ridge and on to the top. We lay on the top of Meall na h' Aisre for an hour in warm sun.

Invasion of England

The next step, in the Prince's view, was the invasion of England and, although the clan chiefs were unenthusiastic, a majority vote was in favour of proceeding. The main worry was how to deal with the formidable Field-Marshal Wade and his army ensconced in Newcastle. Here, Intelligence sources - not for the first or last time - failed the Jacobites as Wade was by now somewhat senile, and his army would not have posed much of a threat. However the decision was taken to go by Carlisle.

A successful tactical plan was evolved by the Jacobites. The Prince led a main division into the Eastern Borders to Kelso in order to give the impression that Newcastle was the objective. At Kelso however, they swung westwards via Jedburgh and Hawick into Upper Liddlesdale and joined up with the other main division under Murray. Murray had led the other main division from Edinburgh via Auchendinny to Peebles along the west slopes of the Moorfoots. From Peebles the route taken was by Broughton and Tweedsmuir to Moffat passing the western slopes of **the Manor Hills** and **the Moffat Hills** en route. Then on to Lockerbie where they soon joined up with the other column from Kelso. The joint force then captured Carlisle and marched on south with remarkable speed considering the mid-winter conditions. But the Jacobite support in the north-west England proved to be disappointingly below what had been expected and although the invasion maintained its momentum to Derby, the fateful decision was taken there to turn back. Had Intelligence sources been more efficient it is possible that the decision would have been to push on. However the Jacobite leaders were unaware of the alarm which reigned further south and retreated.

The Manor Hills

On its march south the Jacobite army left Peebles for Moffat and followed the banks of the River Tweed by Broughton and Drumelzier to Tweedsmuir. From Drumelzier to Tweedsmuir, the army was flanked to the east by Manor valley hills. Most of these hills are either Donalds or Donald Tops but there used to be two Corbetts among them, Cramalt Craig and Broadlaw. Cramalt Craig has now been demoted to he a Donald alone, leaving Broadlaw as the only one with a dual qualification in the group.

I walked and camped on these hills on many occasions in pre-war days but my first deliberate 'Donald' oriented walk was one Sunday afternoon in January when I thought that a short walk would be invigorating. I planned to do the circuit of Drumelzier Law, Glenstivon Dodd, Middle Hill and Taberon Law. The conditions were good for a brisk walk. But, as I approached the top of Dulyard Brae, it started to snow quite heavily. So much so that I had a bit of a struggle to reach the summit of Drumelzier Law. The snowstorm showed no signs of abating and I returned quickly to the car.

The east side of the Manor Valley provided me with an entertaining circular walk. From Peebles up Glen Sax along the old Drove road up to

The 1745 Rising

Kailzie Hill, then a good path to Kirkhope Law and Birkscairn Hill and Stake Law. Good walking conditions lead easily to Dun Rig, White Cleuch Hill, Blackhouse Heights and the two tops of Black Law of which the north east is considered to be the Donald. From here back to White Cleuch Hill and along by Glen Rath Heights and Stob Law to Huddlestone Heights and down to the valley by Preston Law.

Another enjoyable round trip was by the Stanhope burn up to the main ridge. It was a superb winter day when I walked over some icy snow patches to Taberon Law, Middle Hill, Dollar Law and along the ridge to Cramalt Craig cutting down to Hunt Law which proved a very pleasant circular trip.

The Moffat Hills

The invading army continued its march south by Tweedsmuir and the Devil's Beef Tub on to Moffat. To the east of the march line between Tweedsmuir and the Beef Tub lie the group of hills dominated by Hart Fell. Further over is the impressive section with White Coomb the highest of them and indeed the highest of all the Moffat Hills. This side of the group is particularly scenic from the narrow road leading up past the Grey Mare's Tail. I have walked on these hills frequently, beginning at either the Devil's Beef Tub or from a suitable starting point on the Moffat - St.Mary's Loch road.

Prince Charles' army must have passed the shoulder of the ridge leading east to Hart Fell. It was along this ridge that I set out to climb Hart Fell taking in an outlier mentioned in the Donald list; Whitehope Heights which I had not traversed on previous walks. Weather conditions were very pleasant when I passed Annanhead Hill, Great Hill, Chalk Rig Edge and Spout Craig, where one crosses a good path coming up from the south. I reached Whitehope Heights and looked around for a small top called Whitehope Knowe mentioned in Donald's supplementary list. This involved a short diversion by Barry Grain Rig and I eventually came to a small cairn which was situated where the top's coordinates given in the list indicate its location. Honour was satisfied and I continued uneventfully up to Hart Fell itself and returned to my car by the same route .

I prefer to ascend into this group either up the Grey Mare's Tail path or by the striking narrow grassy ridge curving attractively up to Saddle Yoke and Under Saddle Yoke . One Saturday in the grouse shooting season we drove to Capplegill Farm and were pleased to find that we could go on the hills as there was no grouse shooting. Sunshine and wind accompanied us up the Saddle Yoke ridge and we continued along it to Cape Law and Din Law, just above Gameshope Loch. From Din Hill we cut across to the slopes of Hart Fell after having to go a mile up stream to get across the water in spate. The fine ridge of Falcon Craig, Swatte Fell and Nether Comb Craig then followed with great views over to Saddle Yoke. We then enjoyed the steep descent by Black Craig back to Capplegill Farm with extensive views of the Ettrick Hills on the other side of the St.Mary's Loch road.

An equally interesting entry to this group of hills is up the Grey Mare's Tail path to Loch Skeen grimly surrounded by its protecting cliffs. Circling round the Loch leads to the tops of Lochcraig Head, Firthhope Rig and on to Firthybrig Head to the top of White Coomb. I descended by Carrifran Gans to complete the round from the car park at the Grey Mare's Tail.

Another alternative approach I used for this group of hills was from the north side near Talla Reservoir up the Gameshope Burn valley to the ruined cottage. Thence we continued up Great Hill and down to Gameshope Loch. From there the excellent ridge over Ellerscleuch Rig, Garelet Dod, Erie Hill, Lairds Cleuch Rig to Garelet Hill brought me back to my car at Talla.

Retreat to Culloden

The decision to retreat had, naturally, a bad effect on morale but the discipline of the army remained high. Although the weather conditions were severe, the army travelled remarkably fast and Lord George Murray conducted a skilful rearguard action. The River Esk was crossed with difficulty at Longtown and the march continued via

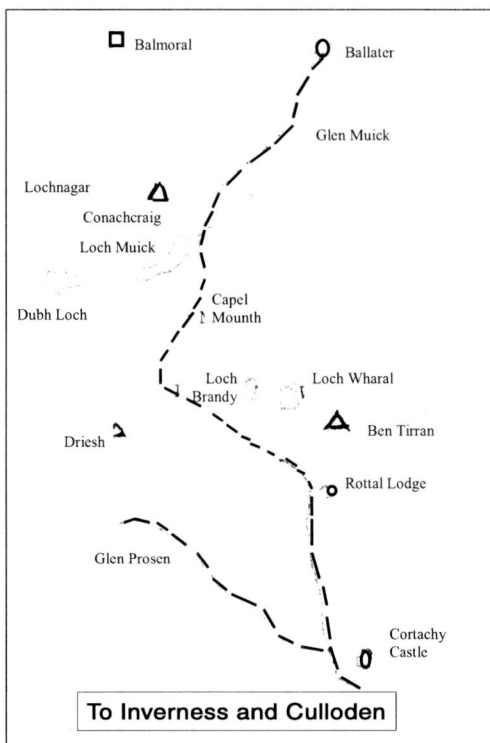

Map 28

The 1745 Rising

Ecclefechan, Annan, Dumfries and Upper Nithsdale where Drumlanrig
Castle was used as a Headquarters for a short time. They then continued
up Nithsdale through the Mennock Pass to Leadhills traversing the slopes
of the Lowther Hills. From there to Douglas with Tinto Hill nearby and
on to Glasgow.

At the same time as the invasion, reinforcements for the Prince had
been accumulating in Scotland and his military position was still quite
strong although Edinburgh had been recaptured for the Government. At
Falkirk, on the way north, the Jacobite army was engaged by Government
forces under General Hawley – a conflict which resulted in a Jacobite
success. But the success was not followed up, and the Government forces
were allowed to regroup. The Jacobites fell back to Perth. From Perth, a
route was taken through Glen Clova and Glen Muick near the slopes of
Corbetts **Ben Tirran** and **Conachcraig** to Speyside and on to Inverness.
(Map 28)

The disastrous finale at Culloden soon followed and the
disappointed Prince was led from the battlefield. Although a material
proportion of the Jacobite army escaped unscathed, its spirit was broken
and its supplies were lost. A final attempt was made to have a rendezvous
of the chiefs at Murlaggan on Loch Arkaig under Corbetts **Fraoch
Bheinn** and **Sgurr Mhurlagain** but there was no hope of reviving the
cause.

Ben Tirran

It was the grouse shooting season when I suggested to Nancy that she
might join me in the climb up Ben Tirran. We obtained permission to go
on the hill even though the present-day Prince Charles had been shooting
there the previous day. I wonder if he realised that his romantic
predecessor Prince Charlie had passed that way nearly 250 years
previously. From Rottal Lodge we set off due north straight up the slope
to the summit .

We were blessed with good weather and had splendid views of Mayar
and Driesh which was a particular pleasure for us both as these two hills
were the last two Munros which Nancy and I and her late husband
George had climbed together. The Glas Maol group and Lochnagar, with
the shapely Corbett Conachcraig, Mounts Keen and Battock and, we
thought, Bennachlie, were all very clear and added to our pleasure at
reaching the top on such a good day.

Conachcraig

Of all the Corbetts and Donalds, this has the most nostalgic memories for me for, as I write this, it is 65 years since I was on its slopes with my Father and my young brother en route to Lochnagar itself - a great thrill for us then. My Father drove us up to Spittal of Glen Muick and we had no route finding problems in reaching the summit of Lochnagar as the sun shone gloriously all day just as it shone for me on Conachcraig 65 years later.

There was one difference however. My Father had no difficulty in parking his car as it was the only one there. To-day I got the last parking place for a long way and counted no less than 60 parked cars. I was astonished to see the area crowded with people and so many facilities available for visitors including a special centre with toilets and a shop. It was gratifying to see so many enjoying the outdoor life. Most were either walking round Loch Muick or enjoying picnicking with their children in the picnic area provided. I certainly met few as I walked up the path to Lochnagar,

At the bealach below Meikle Pap I turned northeast to make the simple climb to Conachcraig. The sun was so warm that I lay at the top enjoying the marvellous views of the surrounding country and did not repeat my ascent to Lochnagar.

Sgurr Mhurlagain and Fraoch Bheinn

Munro and I had intended to have a few days hillwalking in the Glen Dessary country based on A'Chuil. On the way there we estimated that we would have time to climb the two Corbetts above Murlaggan. This isolated place was that chosen for the last rendezvous of the clan chiefs after Culloden to see if there was any possibility of continuing the rising but the spirit was broken and nothing came of it.

We parked the car at the Strathan forestry gate to Glen Dessary. We followed the ridge up the west side of the Dearg Allt and although mist and rain came down the ridge was clearly defined and we had no difficulty in locating the cairn at the top of Fraoch Bheinn. At the cairn we both took compass bearings for Sgurr Mhurlagain and found that, for some reason, both compasses were giving obvious errors of direction. It is with reluctance that one distrusts the compass but on this occasion we had no doubts. However we cautiously descended the ridge by the way we had come up for a short time and were soon able to see the bealach between the two Corbetts below us. We descended to the south end of the fairly broad bealach and found that our compasses were working again. A fairly long ascent up the Sgurr Mhurlagain south west ridge took us directly to the summit cairn. On the way down the mist lifted and we angled off the ridge to reach the delightful path going down the east side of the Allt Dearg. Delightful since we enjoyed direct views up Glens Dessary and Pean, with their memories of Bonnie Prince Charlie in the Heather, and Gulvain, Sgurr Thuilm and the Streaps.

Glen Affric

The Prince in the Heather

From Culloden to Loch nan Uamh

After the battle of Culloden, the Jacobite army moved south to Aviemore and Ruthven where it was eventually dispersed. The Prince also moved south as far as the Mains of Faillie where he crossed the River Nairn and rode on past Loch Dun Seilcheig and Loch Ruthven to Gorthlick on Loch Mhor. Loch Ruthven is now well known as the site of the R.S.P.B. hide for observing Slavonian Grebes. The Prince rode on to Fort Augustus and Invergarry. From there he appears to have ridden along the west bank of Loch Lochy to Clunes, past Achnasaul, to Murlaggan where the final rendezvous for the clan chiefs had been planned. He stayed in this area for several days, at Kinlocharkaig, until the final meeting proved abortive.

135

He walked over the hills up Glen Pean, passing the south slopes of Corbett **Carn Mor** and near to **Sgurr na H'Aide** and on to Meoble in Morar. This rough walk, after the battlefield trauma he had experienced and the long hours of riding he had had, must have left him pretty exhausted. However he walked on down Glen Beasdale to Borradale, the point where he had originally landed all these months ago.

Carn Mor and Sgurr na H'Aide (now known as Bidean a'Chabair)

I had obtained permission from the Forestry Commission to use my car on the private road on the south side of Glen Dessary. This road goes further up the Glen to its terminal point at Allt Coire nan Uth. From here Munro and I decided to tackle Sgurr na h'Aide first. It was really hard work contouring round the lower slopes of Meall nan Spardan. We aimed at a small bealach south west of Druim Coire nan Laoigh. The ascent to this point was very steep and rough and the rough ground continued along the ridge up to the final rise to the summit of Sgurr na h'Aide. The final ascent involved us in some rocky scrambling and we had to descend from the summit in a north-easterly direction to get back to the ridge. The visibility at the summit was limited in scope and, without delay, we retraced our steps along the ridge to the little lochan south west of Druim Coire nan Laoigh. From here we descended by a small stream south-eastwards to the bealach in Gleann an Lochain Eanaiche. From this bealach we climbed up the rocky ridge to the west of Allt Coire an t'Searraich. This took us to the summit ridge of Carn Mor and here we struck an old boundary fence, marked on the map as going to the summit. We followed this along the long ridge which had some frustrating minor tops en route and eventually reached the substantial cairn. Sadly it was by now very wet and misty. From the summit we wanted to descend along the ridge of Meall nan Spardan and in the mist we had to take great care that we did not stray onto the long ridge leading to Monadh Gorm and Strathan. However having satisfied ourselves that we had got it right, we steadily progressed along the ridge which again was rocky. This persisted most of the way down. We ended up in a recently trenched forestry plantation where in our tiring state, the walking was not pleasant. We were glad to have the car at the end of the Forestry road.

The Islands

From Loch nan Uamh the Prince crossed to Benbecula in stormy conditions, which cannot have done much for his morale. There was a plan to get a boat to take him from Stornoway to the Orkneys and accordingly he sailed via Scalpay to Harris. (*Map 29)* Here he landed on the shore of Loch Seaforth and cannot have been far from the only Corbett of the Outer Isles, **Clisham**. At Stornoway the Orkney plan had to be abandoned and he returned via Scalpay and Rodel in Harris to Loch Uskavagh in Benbecula. He spent some time in South Uist but eventually enlisted the help of Flora MacDonald to smuggle him across to Skye. He landed in Skye near Uig in Trotternish and walked to Portree which along with Sligachan was occupied by Government troops. He crossed to Raasay but felt that the island was too small for him to hide on and recrossed to the mainland of Skye. Here he circled round Portree and Sligachan, hugging the shore of the Loch to avoid the troops in the towns. He passed the slopes of one of the Red Cuillin Corbetts, Glamaig, near Sconser and continued to Loch Ainort. From here he walked down Glen Mhor close by the Corbett Garbh-bheinn and reached Elgol - a somewhat roundabout route. At Elgol, the old Chief of the MacKinnons took over responsibility for getting him safely back to the mainland and a boat took them over to Mallaig.

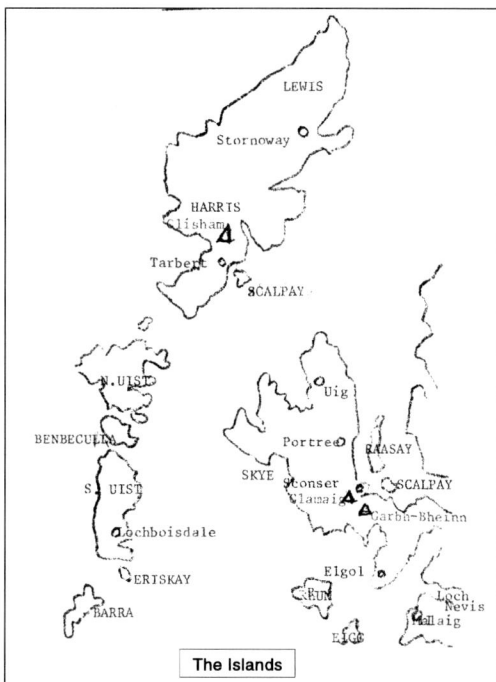

Map 29

Harris
Clisham

The only Corbett in the Outer Hebrides is Clisham, one of a splendid ridge of hills in the north portion of Harris, separating Harris from Lewis. The ascent of Clisham is only a matter of a few hours from the road but to get there is quite an expedition.

After his successful ascent of Beinn Talaidh in Mull, Tom was keen to add to his list and when he heard that I was planning to go to Harris he asked to join me in the ascent of Clisham. We travelled to Skye and crossed from Uig to Tarbert in clear and calm weather via Lochmaddy. The Shiant Isles stood out prominently as we crossed and behind Tarbert we could see the hills including Clisham. It was a Sunday morning when we set out for Clisham through Tarbert streets quite deserted because it was the Sabbath day. We drove up the Stornoway road and in clear and sunny weather parked the car at the bridge over the Maaruig river. We decided to go up onto the south east ridge of Clisham between the Maaruig river and Allt Tomnaval. In a short time we found a line of cairns which we followed to the unmistakable summit ridge and in due course to the summit itself.

North to Glen Affric

After a few nights in the open at Mallaig, the Prince walked by night to Morar and then back once again to Borradale on Loch nan Uamh, where they found that MacDonald's house had been burned down and he was living in a bothy. Reconnaissance revealed the presence of strong Government army and naval forces and the Prince walked back to Meoble. Here they were informed that the Government had heard that the Prince had returned to Moidart and they had established a line of sentinels from Loch Eil to Loch Hourn. The Prince decided to try to break through the line and make for Poolewe. *(Map 30)*

From Meoble, they walked to Sgurr a Mhuidhe and climbed Fraoch-bheinn, the outlier of Corbett **Sgurr an Utha**. The Red Coats were close to them at this stage and so they walked on to Coire Odhar east of Loch Beoraid. A rendezvous was planned on Sgurr nan Coireachan but the proximity of the troops kept the Prince on the move. Contouring the slopes of Corbett **Sgurr Cos na Breachd-laoigh**, they crossed into the head waters of Glen Kingie near Kinbreack with Corbett **Sgurr an Fhuarain** in the hill range ahead of them. They then proceeded to Coire nan Gall, on the east slopes of that magnificent Corbett, **Ben Aden** and near the head of the 'old' Loch Quoich before the level was raised. From here they climbed Druim Chosaidh which is an outlier of Corbett **Sgurr a'Choire-bheithe**. They could see the enemy guards below them and after climbing over the ridge of Corbett **Sgurr nan Eugallt**, they slipped through the line of guards and rested in Coire Sgoir-adail north of Loch Hourn head. There is a track leading over from Loch Hourn via the Bealach Duibh-leac and Coire Mhalagain to Glen Shiel and they crossed over this track and made their way up Glen Shiel. They spent a night on a hill overlooking Strath Cluanie, quite possibly Am Bathach. Their next shelter was a cave on the slopes of Sgurr nan Conbhairean. From this cave they descended to a shelter in Coire Mheadhoin at the head of Coire Dho on the south slopes of **Aonach Shasuinn**.

Nearness of Government troops again forced a move and they crossed to Glen Affric and Strath Glass. The exact route taken by Prince Charles and his party over to Glen Affric is not firmly established but it would

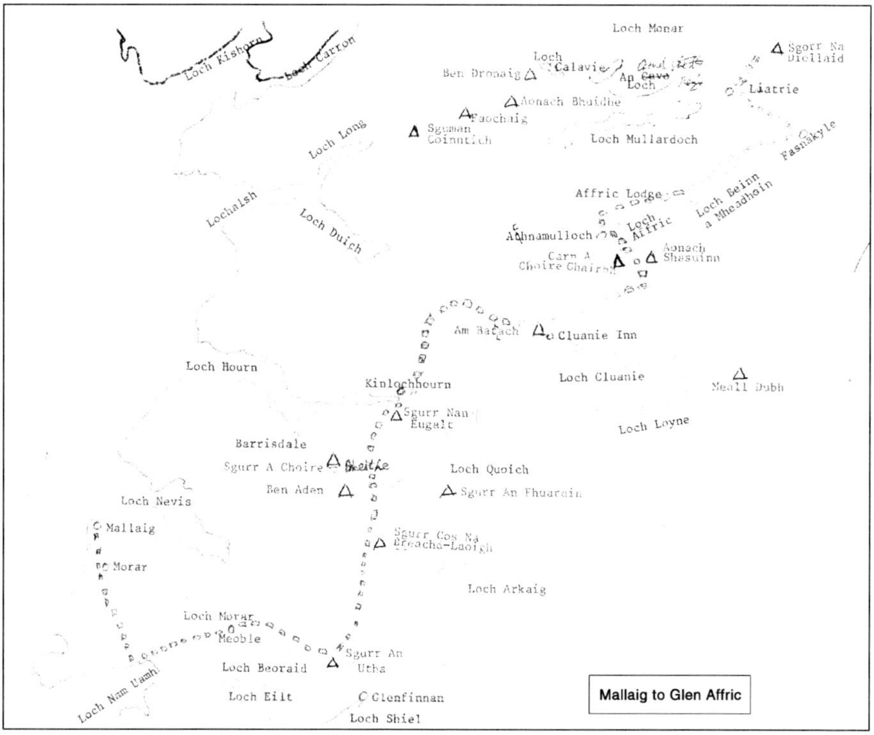

Map 30

most probably be by the Allt na Ciche down to Achnamulloch at the west end of Loch Affric. Conceivably he could have come through by the Allt Garbh to bring him out near Affric Lodge but whichever route was taken, it brought the party close to the Corbetts **Aonach Shasuinn** and **Carn a'Choire Ghairbh.** They continued down Glen Affric to Fasnakyle where the forest afforded good shelter. They then continued north to Glen Cannich and stayed near a farm called Liatrie. While waiting there the Prince climbed Meallan Odhar on the slopes of **Sgorr na Diollaid** to look for his messenger from Poolewe. Shortly, the messenger arrived with the news that the French ship at Poolewe had left for France.

_____

Sgurr an Utha

Hugh and I arrived at Glenfinnan one April afternoon and we walked up Glenfinnan with the ascent of Sgurr an Utha as a possibility. Heavy rain dampened our spirits as we approached Glenfinnan Lodge. The rain was abating slightly as we walked up to inspect the bothy at Corryhully which we found to be in excellent shape. The weather conditions continued to improve and despite the somewhat late hour we decided to make an attempt on Sgurr an Utha. We had reasonably good conditions as we struck straight up the hillside. Sadly mist surrounded us as we reached the summit and so we did not get the hoped for view over Loch Shiel. On the somewhat rocky descent we contoured round Fraoch Bheinn, climbed by the Prince, to reach the road up Glenfinnan over some pretty rough ground.

Sgurr Cos na Breachd - Laoigh

Murray and Sandy and I drove up the shore of Loch Arkaig to Strathan where we parked the cars near the old building reputed to have been used by the sentinels looking out for the Prince. We then walked up Glen Dessary whence we struck out west onto the ridge leading up to the summit ridge which has a number of small subsidiary tops. There was an unexpectedly steep final slope to the summit which we reached in very warm conditions. The visibility was a little hazy but all the Glen Pean and Glen Dessary and Loch Arkaig hills could be identified including Streap and Sgurr an Fhuarain.

Sgurr an Fhuarain

In Glen Kingie, Prince Charlie and his group climbed over into Coire nan Gall to camp near the former head of Loch Quoich. At this stage of their travels they were close to Corbett Sgurr an Fhuarain. Because of the change in level of Loch Quoich, this Corbett is not now so easy of access as it once was.

In the 1930's Jim and I walked through Glenfinnan and then by Allt a Chinn Bhric over to Kinbreack in Glen Kingie. Kinbreack was then occupied by a Cameron stalker, his wife and six children and their resident school-teacher. We reached it in torrential rain and rather than erect our small Black's One Guinea tent, we asked the stalker's permission to sleep in his hay shed. But our request was met by the real old Highland hospitality and he insisted that we should occupy their spare room, and also join them in their evening meal. I have never forgotten that meal, eaten with the portrait of Locheil looking down on us. The old stalker ruled his household firmly and no one, including his wife and the

The Prince in the Heather

The East Knoydart Hills looking over Loch Quoich

schoolteacher, presumed to speak unless spoken to. I must confess that
we two young students were also a bit awestruck. In the morning our
offer of payment for their hospitality was brushed aside with disdain and
we had to resort to sending the family a large box of chocolates when we
got back to Edinburgh. I often wondered how they were shared out.

Access to Gairich and Sgurr an Fhuarain was easy as there was a
good road between the two hills over to Kinlochquoich from where the
stalker's pony could bring in the family provisions. En route to Glen Sheil
we climbed Gairich as we passed but in these days the idea of climbing
Sgurr an Fhuarain, probably only an extra half hour's walk, never entered
our heads. But now much of this road is under the waters of the enlarged
Loch Quoich and access to Sgurr an Fhuarain is not so easy.

Murray, Sandy and I had quite an expedition to get there. Starting
from Invergarry, we drove our cars past Tomdoun to Coille Mhorgil
where we parked. On our cycles we then crossed the river and took a
good forest road for nearly two hours up to Lochan nan Sgud. Here we
left our cycles and walked for about one and a half hours over the south
slopes of Gairich along a rough moorland track until we reached the foot

The Prince in the Heather

of Sgurr an Fhuarain where the old road from Kinbreack came in. Here Sandy decided to start walking back but Murray and I set off up from Coire Ghlais and in a further hour reached the summit of Sgurr an Fhuarain. Splendid views of the hill complexes round Loch Quoich and Glen Kingie were our reward. The descent to our track of approach was uneventful. In the evening sun the descent on our cycles down the forestry road to the cars at Coille Mhargil made a pleasant finish to the walk and a somewhat weary three felt they had earned the drinks they enjoyed at Tomdoun Hotel.

Ben Aden

Ben Aden is not only a Corbett where access demands a considerable effort but it is also unremittingly steep and when the base of the mountain is reached it demands a further considerable effort. I estimated that it would be about six miles in to Barrisdale and about fourteen miles and six thousand feet from Barrisdale and back and then the walk of six miles back to Kinlochhourn.

We arrived at Kinlochhourn at 9 p.m. and were lucky to have a fine cloudless sky for our evening walk in the darkness to Barrisdale along the shores of Loch Hourn. It was of course not possible to relish the fineness of this coastal path but we realised that we would be returning in daylight and could only hope that the weather would remain good for the return journey. We carried tents in case

Kinlochhourn

the bothy at Barrisdale happened to be full when we arrived but when we got there about midnight we were relieved to find that there were only two tents outside the bothy and that the bothy itself was unoccupied. The tide was out in Barrisdale Bay when we arrived and it was unusual to see dimly the deer picking their way over the seaweed covered sands.

The Prince in the Heather

The bothy is almost in the luxury class as far as bothies go and had electric light from the nearby keeper's house until he decides to go to bed.

It was 8 a.m. before we woke to a day of brilliant sunshine. We quickly sorted ourselves out and soon set off along the track up Glen Unndalain looking back from time to time to admire the magnificent Ladhar Bheinn behind us.

The top of the pass released glimpses of Luinne Bheinn and Meall Bhuidhe and of course our main objective, Ben Aden, and Sgurr na Ciche behind it. From the Unndalain bealach the track led down to Lochan nam Breac. From the track the north slope of Ben Aden looked very rough and certainly of unrelenting steepness. Some study through my monocular suggested that a reasonable line would be up the banks of a stream flowing into the east end of Lochan nam Breac. We adopted this route and it was both steep and, in the upper portion, somewhat rocky. The views from the summit on such a fine day were awe-inspiring and fearsome in all directions. No wonder the area is called the Rough Bounds.

Descending was much easier and we were back at Lochan nam Breac by 4 p.m.. By then I had revived enough to contemplate the ascent of Sgurr a Choire - bheithe from the Unndalain bealach ahead of us.

Sgurr a'Choire -beithe

We stopped for sandwiches on the bealach and set off north-east up the very steep outlier of Sgurr a'Choire-bheithe. We reached the ridge fairly soon, where the slopes eased out a good bit. The summit cairn is a good sized one but we didn't stay long there as the weather had now become overcast and cold. We looked along the Druim Chosaidh ridge which Prince Charlie had crossed on his way from Coire nan Gall to the slopes of Corbett Sgurr nan Eugallt and the croft of Kinlochhourn. This must have been a very rough crossing for him as it was probably carried out in darkness. As we elatedly left the summit of our unexpected second Corbett of the day, a heavy snow storm crossed over and without delay we set off for the Unndalain bealach. Perhaps we were a little careless but we got caught up in the steep rocky escarpment to the south-west of the summit. The ground was becoming very slippery and we had to go carefully. In descending a narrow cleft I got jammed and had to take off my rucksack and drop it to the ground some way below. This proved to be a most disappointing action, as although it facilitated my descent, the rucksack fell on very wet ground and my camera with all its irreplaceable photos from the summit of Ben Aden was quite ruined.

The Prince in the Heather

Sgurr nan Eugallt

Murray and I had noticed that a stalker's path was shown on the map as going up from Coireshubh to the bealach between Sgurr Dubh and Sgurr nan Eugallt. We therefore drove along the side of Loch Quoich to little Loch Coire Shubh and parked the car beside the bothy there. We had no trouble finding the stalker's path and, in excellent weather conditions, quickly reached the ridge. The ridge is a really splendid one from the scenic point of view. With a little easy but enjoyable scrambling we reached the summit in about two and a quarter hours.

As a view point I would rate this hill highly in any list of Corbetts arranged in order of the excellence of their summit views. Few could match a view with Beinn Sgritheall and its satellites to the north-west with Skye itself in the distance; all the great Glen Shiel ridges including the Saddle to the north and north-east; the Loch Quoich trio dominating the east view with the shapely Ben Tee standing out well in the distance and of course the grandeur of the roughness of the Knoydart hills to the south.

Our scenic enjoyment continued as we steadily wended our way back to the the bealach and the path which we were glad to pick up for the descent to the car.

Aonach Shasuinn and Carn a'Choire Ghairbh

I drove to the east end of Loch Affric and, from the car park there, cycled along the south side of the loch to a bridge over the Allt Garbh where there were indications of a path going up the east side of the stream crossing over in a short distance. However the path became somewhat indistinct, to put it mildly, and I could find no suitable place to cross the stream, which was running pretty full, to enable me to climb Carn Glaslochdarach. So the east bank of the Allt Garbh was followed up to Loch an Sguid and very coarse walking it was. If this was typical of the Prince's sheltering countryside in this part of the world, then it was no wonder that he was not spotted by the red-coats. From Loch an Sguid I aimed at the west summit of Aonach Shasuinn and proceeded from there to the main east summit having taken considerably longer than I had calculated. Although it was overcast, the cloud base was high and I traversed round to the bealach below Carn a Choire Ghairbh . From the summit I trudged down the broad ridge to Carn Glaslochdarach and then descended a steep rocky escarpment to the new forestry plantations below. I soon picked up a good forestry road leading me back to my cycle and on to the car.

The Prince in the Heather

Sgurr na Diollaid

Sgurr na Diollaid

This was the most northerly Corbett reached by Prince Charles. He had been living at a farm in Glen Cannich called Liatrie, awaiting a messenger from Poolewe with news of a French ship expected there. He climbed Meallan an Odhar, the outlier of Sgurr na Diollaid to see if he could see any sign of the messenger.

I climbed Sgurr na Diollaid in a combined operation with Wilf. He dropped me off at Muchrachd in Glen Cannich while he continued to the Mullardoch dam to climb the Munros round there. I walked due north from the road junction but there were no paths and I had to force my way through thick heather and peat bogs. The final summit ascent itself was surprisingly rocky and I found that there were two peaks. I reached the southern one in two and a quarter hours but I found the direct approach to the northern one too precipitous and I had to circle round to make an easy ascent from the south side. The views were hazy but the Sgurr na Lapaich-An Riabhachan ridge above Loch Mullardoch where Wilf was walking was well clear. I returned uneventfully to the road and waited patiently until Wilf appeared from Loch Mullardoch.

The Prince in the Heather

South to Badenoch

On receipt of the Poolewe information the Prince decided to turn south. He crossed the River Cannich near Muchrachd and rested again at Fasnakyle. A cross country route then took him over by Guisachan and Loch na Beinne Baine to Glen Moriston. They forded the River Moriston and walked up Glen Loyne, and, after fording the River Garry with difficulty, proceeded to Achnasaul.(*Map 31*)

Several days were spent in this area discussing plans with Lochiel and others and the Prince camped on the slopes of Meall an Tagraidh, an outlier of Corbetts **Meall na h'Eilde** and **Geal Charn**. Finally the decision was taken to move to Badenoch . The River Lochy was crossed and the eastern shore of Loch Oich was followed until they could cut up into Glen Tarf as Montrose had done before them in his epic march to Inverlochy, and then by the shoulder of Carn Leac, probably down the Allt Chonnal into the head waters of Glen Roy. Following the River Roy to near its source would then bring them to the famous 'window' of Coire Ardair and down to to Aberarder on Loch Laggan. They would then walk along to Kinloch Laggan and turn south towards Meallan Odhar near Loch Pattack. Cluny's clansmen contacted them there and they repaired to the famous Cage on Ben Alder where no doubt they would receive a great welcome from Cluny MacPherson.

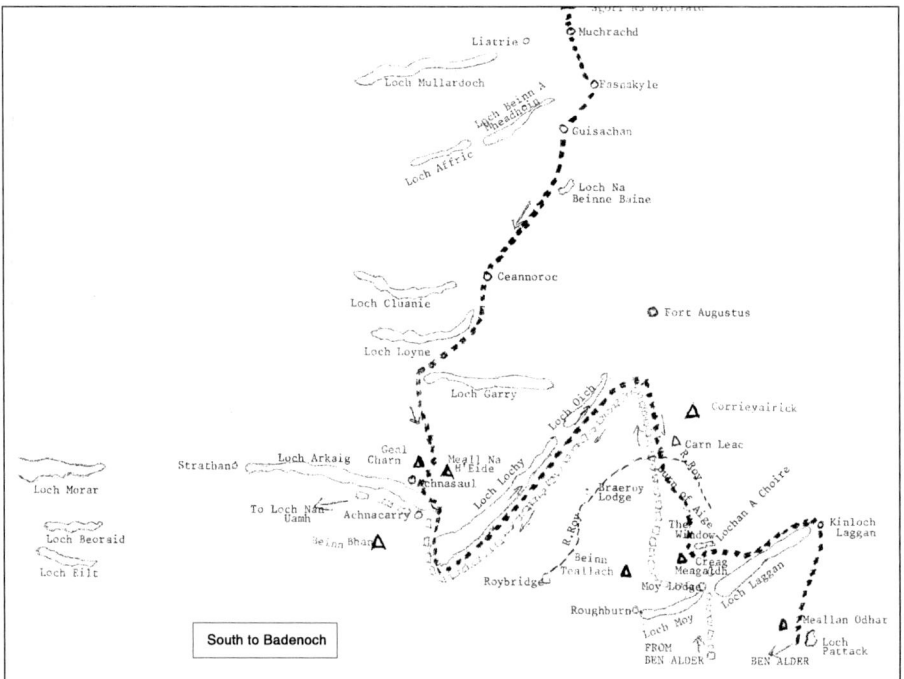

Map 31

The Prince in the Heather

Meall na h'Eilde and Geal Charn

While waiting to meet Lochiel at Achnasaul, Prince Charles sheltered on the slopes of Meall an Tagraidh. So he almost certainly climbed Meall na h'Eilde though he is unlikely to have walked along the ridge to Geal Charn as he would be too exposed to view.

By starting at Achnasaul as we did we may have followed in the footsteps of the Prince . We took the rough track up the east side of the Allt Dubh to a point beyond Beinn Mheadhoin where we followed a north - west bearing to the summit of Geal Charn. As the map indicates, this is a really fine view point and we lingered happily at the cairn picking out all the favourite tops; Ben Nevis and its cliffs, the Grey Corries, parts of the Mamores and parts of Glencoe's hills, the Loch Treig group (including Corbett Leum Uilleim), the Ben Alder hills, the hills of Glen Dessary, Glen Shiel, Glen Finnan and Ardgour. All were wonderfully clear and distinct and even further away more ranges could be seen but too indistinct to pinpoint with certainty. One of the really superb Corbett view points.

A thousand feet of ascent took us onto the top of Meall Choire nan Saobhaidh and then onto the summit of Meall na h'Eilde. We descended by the steep ridge leading to the head of Gleann Cia-aig where a bridge in the gully put us onto a good forestry track leading down to the main road.

The Final Time at Loch nan Uamh

News of a French ship at Loch nan Uamh reached the Cage and, saying farewell to Cluny, who remained there for a further nine years, they set off to the west. They walked to Moy Lodge and then probably along to Roughburn to pass through to Glen Roy by the Allt a Chaoruinn and then the Burn of Agie. This route would take them over the slopes of Corbett (now promoted to Munro) **Beinn Teallach**. They then retraced their steps over Carn Leac to Glen Tarf and along the shores of Loch Oich and Loch Lochy to reach Locheil at Achnacarry, under the slopes of Corbett **Beinn Bhan**. At Achnacarry, the ship's presence in Loch nan Uamh was confirmed. Taking what by then must have been a somewhat familiar route they reached the Loch safely for the final time and embarked for France.

Beinn Teallach

I walked up the Allt a'Chaoruinn valley from Roughburn with the intention of cutting up onto the long south shoulder of the hill. Unfortunately I went too far up the valley and landed myself on a very steep rocky scramble to the summit ridge by then in mist. I struck the ridge at a point quite close to the summit. The mist suddenly cleared and I had splendid views, not only of Ben Chaoruinn to the east and the Glen Roy hills to the west but also the fine hills to the south particularly those around Loch Treig. The clear visibility enabled me to find an easy path down the south shoulder and I had no difficulty crossing the Allt a Chaoruinn to get onto its eastern bank for the return to Roughburn.

Beinn Bhan

Munro and I did not climb Beinn Bhan from Achnacarry but drove round from Gairlochy to Glen Loy and parked at the deserted farmhouse of Inverskilavuilin. From here we found a path which took us a good long way up the west side of Monadh Uisge Mhuillin. At this stage we found ourselves in mist and had to use compasses to get the north west bearing we needed. The ridge is a very broad one and we were lucky to find the summit cairn fairly quickly. A straightforward descent took us back to the car .

Beinn Damh

Queen Victoria's Scottish Expeditions

The progresses of the Stewart monarchs, the foot pilgrimages of
James IV to St. Ninian's shrine in Whithorn, the circumnavigation of
Scotland by James V in his fleet, the peregrinations by Bonnie Prince
Charlie after Culloden are previous examples of Scottish royalty
journeying around Scotland. But Queen Victoria's travels in her long
reign must, I feel, for quantity and variety although perhaps not for
endurance of hardships like Prince Charlie, give her first place among
those of Royal blood for their travels in Scotland. Her female
predecessor, Mary Queen of Scots, travelled widely around Scotland in
the first few years of her reign but these travels were largely associated
with her judicial duties and probably also with the political motive of
improving her personal image among the people in times where personal
appearances were the only method of achieving this end. With Queen
Victoria however, it was her real love for the Scottish countryside and the
Scottish people which motivated her - a love fortunately shared by her

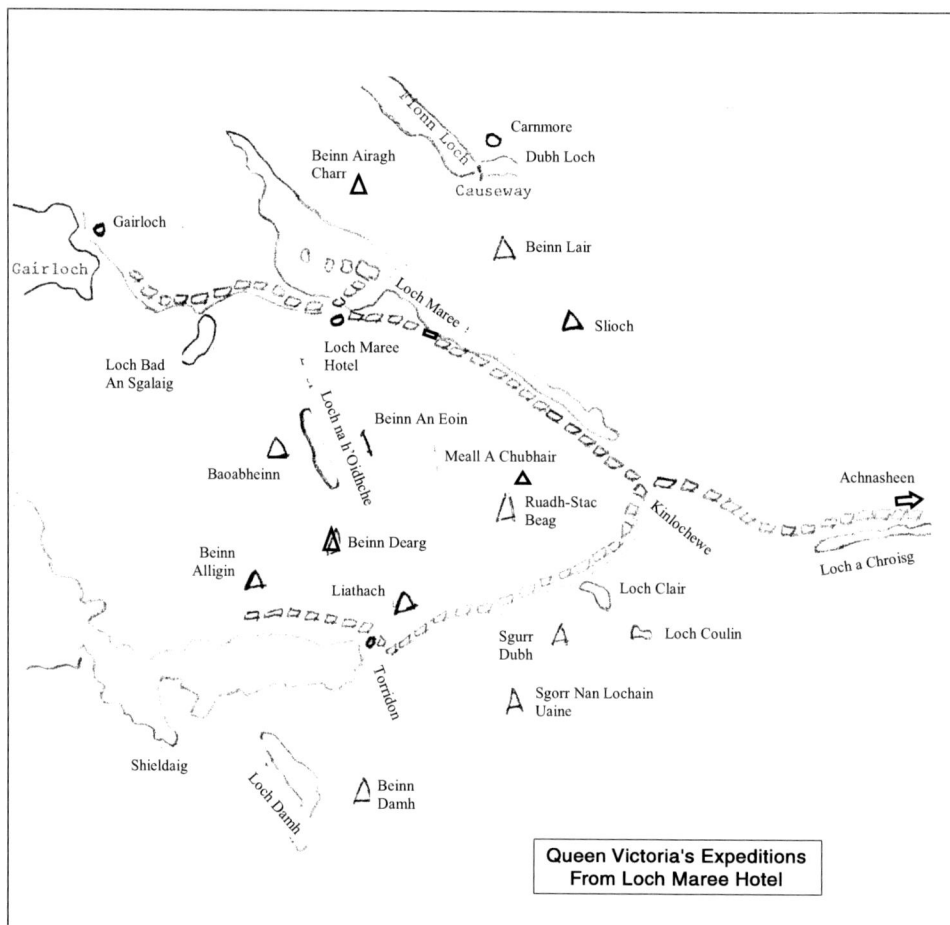

Beinn Airagh
Charr

Carnmore

Dubh Loch

Causeway

Beinn Lair

Fionn Loch

Gairloch

Gairloch

Loch Maree

Slioch

Loch Bad
An Sgalaig

Loch Maree
Hotel

Beinn An Eoin

Loch na h'Oidhche

Baoabheinn

Meall A Chubhair

Achnasheen

Beinn Dearg

Ruadh-Stac
Beag

Kinlochewe

Loch a Chroisg

Beinn
Alligin

Liathach

Loch Clair

Sgurr
Dubh

Loch Coulin

Torridon

Sgorr Nan Lochain
Uaine

Shieldaig

Loch Damh

Beinn
Damh

**Queen Victoria's Expeditions
From Loch Maree Hotel**

Map 32

consort Prince Albert. Her visit to Scotland in 1842 was, apart from the isolated visit of George IV in 1822, the first by a reigning monarch from London since Charles I.

It is fascinating to read in her diaries of the numerous expeditions which were organised on her behalf. It is quite astonishing how many Munros she ascended, admittedly with the assistance of ponies, but even more astonishing is her knowledge of the countryside revealed from the summits she reached. Like all of us, she enjoyed picking out the other hills and ranges she recognised.

Queen Victoria's Scottish Expeditions

Of particular interest to me was her expedition to the West Highlands. (*Map 32*). The expedition commenced with a train journey from Ballater to Aberdeen and then across by Keith and Elgin to Inverness and on to Dingwall. Here they left the main line north and traveled west by Strathpeffer and Strath Bran to Achnasheen. Here the royal party left the train and transferred to horse drawn transport. They followed the road to the north of Loch a Chroisg where the Queen remarks on the view to the high peaks of Corbett Sgurr a Mhuillin. The route continued down Glen Docherty along the south side of Loch Maree where the Queen described in glowing terms the beauties of Slioch and its surroundings. Their residence for the expedition was the Loch Maree Hotel.

The following day the Queen walked part of the way back to Kinlochewe and was greatly impressed by the magnificent peaks all around them which must have included Corbetts **Ruadh-stac Beag** and **Meall a'Ghuibhas**, the northern outliers of Beinn Eighe.

On her second day at the Loch Maree Hotel, the Queen decided on an outing to Loch Torridon. The route took the party past Loch Clair whose charm was recorded by the Queen - as by many others after her. She referred to the high hills behind the loch which would include Corbetts Sgurr Dubh and Sgor an Lochain Uaine. As with most people also the great peak of Liathach made a profound impression on her Majesty who continued her outing along to the end of Upper Loch Torridon. At this point she refers to the high peak of Corbett **Beinn Damh** to the south and the great range of hills to the north which would include Corbett **Beinn Dearg**.

On the third day the Queen was rowed out to Eilan Maree and noted the striking range of hills rising from the north shore of the Loch which comprise Corbetts, **Beinn Airigh Charr** and **Beinn Lair.** The Queen did not fail to refer to the historical associations of the island with Saint Maelrubhe whose penetration to this area I have already referred to. Her final expedition from Loch Maree Hotel was to Kerrie's Bridge near Gairloch where the Queen had heard that a large party had taken the trouble to sail over from Stornoway in Lewis for the purpose of seeing their 'beloved Queen'. The Queen felt that she must not disappoint them and received a warm welcome from them. From this road the Queen must have looked at and admired the great peaks of Corbetts **Baosbheinn** and **Beinn an Eoin** to the south.

The Queen must have really enjoyed this expedition as, in her Diary, she expresses the hope that some day she will be able to return to the Loch Maree Hotel.

Beinn Dearg from Loch na h'Oidche

Ruadh-Stac Beag and Meall a'Guibhais

The slopes of these two Corbetts are clearly seen from the road along which Queen Victoria walked from the Loch Maree Hotel. From the map we decided to start near the Nature Reserve Hut at Anancaun where a pony track led up into the Beinn Eighe massif. As it was possible that some deer-culling might be in progress I phoned up the Nature Reserve Office the night before to ascertain that it would be in order to walk on the hills the next day and was glad to hear that there was no difficulty.

As we got up the hill we decided to follow the easterly track leading to Beinn Eighe and contour round to the bealach between Sgurr Bhan and Ruadh-stac Beag. It proved very difficult going up the steep rocky ascent to the Ruadh-stac Beag summit. The wind gusts were very severe and several times we were completely unbalanced. At the Ruadh-stac Beag summit we wondered if the descent to the bealach under Meall a'Ghuibhais would give us similar problems. However the descent proved surprisingly quick and we proceeded to climb the slope to Meall a'Ghuibhais - rather a steep slope with which to finish.

The Torridon Corbetts
Beinn Damh

Murray and I decided to start this walk from the Loch Torridon Hotel and we parked the car at the side of the road and found a wicket gate leading to a path through the fine woods above the hotel. It was a glorious day of sunshine and the walk through the pine woods with rhododendron bushes and a splendid stream foaming along down below made time pass quickly until we emerged from the forest. Our aim was the portion of the main ridge between Sgurr na Bana Mhoraire and the main top of Beinn Damh and we soon reached this objective and continued along the ridge with Coire Toll Ban on our left. Following the ridge in a south east direction we were disappointed to find a thick mist spreading along the ridge. The route was, however, well cairned and we followed them along bypassing subsidiary tops. We eventually came to a large cairn and thought that we had reached the summit when we suddenly saw a figure appearing out of the mist. He turned out to be a German visitor who promptly told us that we were not at the summit and that it was the next top. The ridge to the final top was fairly narrow but the cairn was clearly the top one. We turned back along the proper compass bearing and to our delight the mist cleared away and we got fine views of the whole Torridon hill range .

Beinn Dearg

This is a really splendid hill and its failure to attain Munro status by a few feet has meant that it has not received the attention that its mighty three neighbours have had. It is of course not so readily accessible as the big three but on a day of good visibility it would probably rank superior to its Munro companions as they would all three be included in its panorama as well as the lesser hills around.

Frances, Munro and I took the path up the bank of the Abhainn Coire Mhic Nobuil and continued along this path admiring the cliff faces of Beinn Dearg until we reached a point slightly south west of Carn Feola. Here we followed a small stream and reached the ridge, in mist alas, slightly to the west of Carn Feola. The initial stages of the ridge were fairly straightforward but there followed a few rocky steps quite exposed to the north where we bypassed the crest of the ridge on the south side. We had a little difficulty in the mist in locating the summit cairn and as the mist was still thick and the much anticipated view was not forthcoming we carefully retraced our steps along the ridge and descended with no difficulty.

Beinn Airigh Charr and Beinn Lair

Having carried to Carnmore about 40 pounds each in our rucksacks including our lightweight tents and food for four days we decided to utilise one of the days for climbing Beinn Airigh Charr and Beinn Lair. We crossed the causeway between Fionn Loch and Dubh Loch and followed a path leading to Bealach Mheinnidh.

The views of Beinn Lair as we ascended this path are very different indeed from those which entranced Queen Victoria from Eilan Maree. From the Loch, Beinn Lair must seem a gentle hill rising from a delightfully wooded base but from the Bealach Mheinnidh path there can be seen one of the finest of cliff faces in the country running north west to south east. The highest point of the hill is about midway along the cliff range and is in the centre of a fairly large plateau but although it could be difficult to locate in mist, there is a pretty large cairn to mark it. From the bealach there is an easy grassy slope, skirting the edge of the cliffs all the way to the summit. At one stage there is a view point where one can really enjoy the views of the great cliff face and of course the Fionn Loch and the Dubh Loch and indeed we could see our tiny tents.

From the top we decided to descend almost due west. There is a hill path leading over from Letterewe to Carnmore which we had used in reaching Bealach Meinnidh and off this path a track leads first north west and then north to Beinn Airigh Charr, crossing round Meall Mheinnich in the process. On this route we obtained splendid views of Loch Maree and its islands. When we reached the path we enjoyed another easy grassy ascent to the summit of Beinn Airigh Charr where the sun was shining and the visibility perfect. We spent some time enjoying a rare view of the Great Wilderness and its well known peaks and lochs. To the south, when we had reached an appropriate height, we were regaled by glorious views of the Torridon hills. For our descent, as the weather conditions were so good we took a somewhat steep descent almost south east to bring us out at the bridge over the Strathan Buidhe. From here we followed the route back to the causeway and the tents.

Beinn an Eoin and Baosbheinn

The final expedition made by Queen Victoria took her near to the remote and wild country in which Corbetts Beinn an Eoin and Baosbheinn are to be found.

We parked our car at Loch Bad an Scalaig, about four and a half miles from Gairloch. We then carried our packs a further four miles up to Loch na h'Oidhche at whose northern end there is a small boat hut. The hut was unoccupied and reasonably clean and in order to save time in the morning we decided to sleep on the concrete floor in our sleeping bags and not erect our small tents. We had an early start leaving our sleeping and cooking gear in the hut.

There are no paths in this wild area and without more ado we took to the slope up the north west ridge of Beinn an Eoin. The ridge is straightforward with a series of minor tops which as usual made me wonder when we would come to the real one. A steep final ascent and then a pretty narrow ridge took us on the top. A pathless rough descent saw us at the Poca Buidhe, a fisherman's cottage at the south end of Loch na h'Oidhche.

Passing Gorm Loch na Beinne we traversed wet and boggy ground to the south east end of Baosbheinn. Route finding on this hill was a little confusing as there are a few minor tops on the way up. The visibility at the summit had deteriorated and there was a covering of mist on the ridge. We did not delay but started our descent to the boat hut to collect the belongings we had left there. We were a little worried that we would not be able to get over the stream flowing out of Loch na h'Oidhche as it had looked to be flowing pretty fully when we left in the morning.

Although we would have liked to complete the ridge of this fine hill we decided to make a direct descent to the boat hut from the ridge. In the mist we made an unsuccessful attempt and had to turn back as the going was too precipitous and we could not see where it was leading us. Our second attempt was more successful and we reached the stream which we were able to negotiate somewhat above knee level and returned to our base safely.

Broadlaw

The Final Corbett and Donald

There were a number of reasons why I had left Broadlaw as the final climb. Firstly I hoped that a number of my grandchildren would be able to come and, as there is a good road up Broadlaw, it would be well within the powers of them all, even the youngest. Secondly some of my friends who had joined me on some of the walks during the last few years were resident in England as were two of my grandchildren, and Broadlaw is conveniently situated from the access point of view both for Scottish and English participants.

Another reason was that I was born in a house with a garden running down to the River Tweed and I thought I would like a hill also on the edge of the Tweed to be my final hill. Yet another reason was that Broadlaw can rank both as one of Corbett's list and also as one of Donald's list so that I could finish both lists with the one climb.

For such an occasion when so many of my friends were taking the trouble to come and walk the final hill with me, it was desirable to have a suitable hostelry in order to offer some hospitality as a mark of my appreciation. Naturally the Crook Inn was eminently suitable for this purpose. But a reason which romantically attracted me was very much in my mind. It was at the Crook Inn that the Scottish Mountaineering Club held its first meet exactly a hundred years previously. The hospitality of the Inn had been enjoyed on that occasion and Broadlaw was climbed by the members.

For these various reasons Broadlaw had seemed the ideal hill to end the lists and I therefore visited Mr. Dempster, farmer of Hearthstane Farm over whose land the party would be walking to ensure that he had no objections to the expedition. When the circumstances were explained he most willingly agreed to the invasion. At the Crook Inn I received the fullest cooperation and a suitable meal was organised. It was also arranged that we might have the use of changing rooms for ladies and gentlemen returning from the walk before the meal. This proved a great blessing on account of the inclement weather.

Broadlaw – the Final Corbett and Donald

It was a great pleasure for me that so many of my immediate family made the effort to climb the final hill with me and it was a particular surprise that my daughter and her son from Switzerland flew over specially. I was also honoured that so many of the friends who had climbed with me came along, some of them from well south in England. The only disappointment was that the weather was atrocious and the rain came down incessantly. However everyone braved the elements although there was no hope of any view.

We assembled in the car park of the Crook Inn and set off for Hearthstane Farm crossing the River Tweed, much smaller here than it is at my place of birth. A good path follows the north banks of the Hearthstane Burn and later the Glen Heurie Burn onto the north-west slopes of Broadlaw. In terrible conditions, we continued beyond the substation buildings to the true top and then returned to the shelter of the buildings to consume a welcome glass of champagne and some cake.

We did not tarry however and the bedraggled party wended its way back to the Crook Inn where a warm welcome and changing rooms awaited the party. The Inn had prepared a most acceptable meal and in my 'Thank-you' remarks I mentioned that Sir Hugh Munro and his mountaineering friends had experienced similarly bad weather in 1888. The great pleasure that I had, in seeing present so many splendid friends who had helped me along more than made up for my disappointment that I had selected a day of such bad weather.

When I was climbing these hills I always had at the back of my mind the possibility of writing a book donating all profits to charity. Thus, although there is always a feeling of emptiness on completion of a project, I knew I would get much enjoyment in writing up the details and reliving the ascents that I could no longer physically make. I would also be left with a host of happy memories of the many superb companions with whom I had shared the enjoyment of these great Scottish hills.

REFERENCES

ANDERSON: St. Ninian. The Faith Press.
G.W.S. BARROW: Kingship and Unity. Scotland 1000-1306. New History of Scotland. Edward Arnold Ltd.
BAYNES: The Jacobite Rising of 1715. Cassell and Co.
C. BINGHAM: The Stewart Kingdom of Scotland. Weidenfeld & Nicolson.
BLACK: Culloden and the 1745. St.Martins Press,
BLAIKIE: Itinerary of Prince Charles Edward Stuart. Constable.
R. L. BREMNER: The Norsemen in Alba. Maclehose,Jackson & Co..
H. M. BROWN: Climbing the Corbetts. Gollancz.
H. M. BROWN: The Island of Rum. Guide Book .
JOHN BUCHAN: Cromwell. Reprint Society.
JIM CRUMLEY: A High and Lonely Place. Jonathan Cape.
DAVID DAICHES: Scotland and the Union. John Murray Ltd., London.
DICK: Highways and Byways in Galloway and Carrick. MacMillan & Co
DICKSON: The Jacobite Attempt of 1719. Scottish History Society
G. DONALDSON: The Edinburgh History of Scotland. Oliver and Boyd.
F. D. DOW: Cromwellian Scotland 1651-1660. John Donald Ltd.
DAVID DUFF: Victoria in the Highlands. Muller
DAVID DUFF: Queen Victorials Highland Journals. Webb & Bower.
ELLIS: Macbeth. Frederick Muller Ltd.
LENMAN EYRE: The Jacobite Risings in Britain 1689-1746. Methuen
FORSTER: The Rash Adventurer. Secker and Warburg
DUNCAN FRASER: Highland Perthshire. Montrose Standard Press.
FUMEAUX: The Agricola of Tacitus.
VICTOR GAFFNEY: The Lordship of Strathavon. Aberdeen University Press.
GEOGRAPHICAL SOCIETY: The Early Maps of Scotland. Constable.
I. F. GRANT: The Lordship of the Isles. The Moray Press
I. F. GRANT: Angus Og of the Isles. W.& R. Chambers Ltd.
I. F. GRANT: The Macleods. Spurbooks.
I. F. GRANT: In the Tracks of Montrose. Maclehose Ltd.,London.
I. F. GRANT & HUGH CHEAPE: Periods in Highland History. Shepherd-Walwyn
GRAY: William Wallace. The King's Enemy. Robert Hale, London.
GREGORY: History of the Western Highlands and Islands. John Donald
H.M.S. OFFICE: A Queens Progress. Historic Buildings & Monuments.
KERR: Queen Victoria's Scottish Diaries. Lochar Publishing.
ANDREW LANG: A History of Scotland. William Blackwood and Sons.

References

LANG SYNE PUBLISHERS: Scottish Battles. Glasgow.
LINKLATER & HESKETH:For King and Conscience. Weidenfeld & Nicolson.
LYNCH: Scotland. A New History.   Century Ltd.
D.J.MACDONALD of CASTLETON: Clan MacDonald. Macdonald Publishers.
MACDONALD: Clan Ranald of Knoydart and Glengarry. Dryden Printing Co..
NORMAN MACDOUGALL: James IV. John Donald Ltd.
JAMES A. MACKAY: Robert Bruce, King of Scots . Hale & Co.
FITZROY MACLEAN: A Concise History of Scotland. Thames & Hudson.
INNES MACLEOD: Discovering Galloway. John Donald Ltd..
J. D. MACKIE: A History of Scotland. Allen Lane.
McNEILL & NICHOLSON: An Historical Atlas of Scotland. c400-cl600. St.
Andrew's University Printers.
PETER MARREN: Grampian Battlefields. Aberdeen University Press.
MISCELLANIA SCOTICA: H262 21a   (1583)
MITCHELL GARDNER: History of the Highlands and Gaelic Scotland.
MOODY: Scottish Local History. Batsford Ltd.
MORTON: Galloway and the Covenanters. Gardner.
AGNES MURE MACKENZIE: The Rise of the Stewarts. Oliver & Boyd Ltd
W. H. MURRAY: West Highlands of Scotland. Collins.
NICHOLSON: Edward III and the Scots. Oxford University Press.
PATERSON: Wallace and his Times. W. P.Nimmo.
PINKERTON: History of Scotland preceding 1056. Ballantyne and Co.
A. POLSON: The Book of Ross Sutherland and Caithness. Inverness.
JOHN PREBBLE: The King's Jaunt. Collins.
RAMSAY: The Arrow of Glen Lyon. John Murray.
N. H. REID: Scotland in the Reign of Alexander III. John Donald Ltd.
GRAEME RITCHIE: The Normans in Scotland. Edinburgh University Press
JOHN F. ROBERTSON: The Story of Galloway.   Maxwell,Castle Douglas.
Rev. CHARLES ROGERS: The Book of Wallace. Printed for Grampian Club
Dr. A. B. SCOTT: Scot. Historical Review Vol.Vl pp 260 -280
Dr. A. B. SCOTT: The Pictish Nation.
SCOTTISH HISTORICAL REVIEW: xxxix 1960 pp 98-111. Battle of Carham
SCOTTISH HISTORICAL REVIEW: lv 1976 pp 20-28. Battle of Carham
SCOTTISH HISTORY SOCIETY: Scotland and the Protectorate. 1899
SMYTH: Warlords and Holy Men. New History of Scotland Arnold Ltd.
S. M. C. GUIDE: Munro's Tables and lesser Heights. 1981 Edition,
S. M. C. DISTRICT GUIDE: Southern Uplands, Andrew and Thrippleton.
S. M.. C. HILL WALKERS GUIDE: The Corbetts and Other Hills.
SIMPSON: The Celtic Church in Scotland. Aberdeen University Press.
SIMPSON: The Historical St.Columba. Oliver and Boyd.
SIMPSON: Proc. Soc.Ant.Scot.Vol,LX1V pp48-52

References

STEWART ROSS: Monarchs of Scotland. Lochar Publishing.
RALPH STORER: Exploring Scottish Hill Tracks. David and Charles.
NIGEL TRANTER: The Lord of the Isles.   Hodder and Stoughton.
JOHN URE: A Bird on the Wing. Constable and Co.Ltd..
I & K WHYTE: On the Trail of the Jacobites. Routledge.
WILSON and GILBERT: The Big Walks. Diadem
WILSON and GILBERT: The Classic Walks. Diadem
WILSON and GILBERT: The Wild Walks.   Diadem.

Index

Index

Index

Index

Index

———

Index

Index

_____